Motivating
Political Morality

Motivating Political Morality

Robert E. Goodin

BLACKWELL
Cambridge MA & Oxford UK

First published 1992

Blackwell Publishers
Three Cambridge Center
Cambridge, Massachusetts 02142
USA

108 Cowley Road
Oxford OX4 1JF
UK

Library of Congress Cataloging-in-Publication Data
Goodin, Robert E.
   Motivating Political Morality / Robert E. Goodin.
      p.   cm.
   'Leiden lectures on law and public policy, Rijksuniversiteit,
   Leiden, the Netherlands, April 1989' –
   Includes bibliographical references (p.   ) and index.
   ISBN 1–55786–247–8 (acid-free paper) – ISBN
   1–55786–332–6 (acid-free paper)
   1. Political ethics.   I. Title.   II. Title: Leiden lectures on
law and public policy.
JA79.G643   1992
172 – dc20   91–41747
                                                        CIP

British Library Cataloguing in Publication Data
A CIP catalogue record for this book is available from the British Library.

Typeset in 11/12 Linotron Palatino
by CentraCet, Cambridge
Printed in Great Britain by
Biddles Ltd., Guildford and King's Lynn

This book is printed on acid-free paper

Contents

Acknowledgments

This book has its origins in a series of public lectures, sponsored by the Leyden Institute for Law and Public Policy – the Onderzoekscentrum Sturing van de Samenleving – at the Rijksuniversiteit Leiden, delivered there in April 1989. It is a pleasure to record my gratitude to Wim Derksen and his colleagues for their genial hospitality and their spirited reactions. These arguments also benefited from subsequent, briefer airings at meetings of the Rationality Group in London and at the Department of Government of the University of Texas in Austin.

The present draft has been shaped by the comments, then and later, of Brian Barry, Patrick Dunleavy, Jon Elster, Amitai Etzioni, James Fishkin, Debbie Fitzmaurice, Paul 't Hart, Hans Keman, Andreas Kinniging, Aat Peterse, Kees Schuyt, Robert van der Veen, Romke van der Veen, Herman van Gunsteren, Hugh Ward, and Willem Witteveen. Mark Bovens, David Miller, and Alan Ryan have been particularly helpful, providing in some cases virtual line-by-line commentaries on the manuscript as a whole.

No doubt I ended up neglecting even more good advice than I ended up taking. Naturally, I alone am responsible for such errors as remain – or at least for those not directly attributable to Brett Goodin's fledgling attempts at composition. His typing will improve. My arguments may not.

Robert E. Goodin
Canberra

Introduction

ONE

Motives, Moral and Otherwise

The central concern of this book is with how best to motivate moral behavior in politics. That problem admits of various formal characterizations, some of which will be elaborated in due course. Let us begin, though, by trying to evoke the general sense of the issue more anecdotally.

Consider the example of Patrick Henry. He is remembered today mainly as the firebrand famous for declaiming, on the eve of the American Revolution, "Give me liberty or give me death!" Patrick Henry was himself a slaveowner, though. He saw the irony. He knew owning slaves was wrong; he admitted as much. "I will not, I cannot, justify it," he said – adding that he was just "drawn along by the general inconvenience of living here [in colonial Virginia] without them."[1] Thomas Jefferson, likewise, found himself writing in the American Declaration of Independence "that man's rights were 'inalienable' at the very same moment when he owned several dozen souls."[2]

The difficulty with Patrick Henry and Thomas Jefferson lay not in persuading them of the right moral principles. They had a keen appreciation of those already. The difficulty lay instead in persuading them to *act* upon those principles. And that, quintessentially, is the problem of motivating moral behavior.

That problem takes many forms, of course, not all of which

1 Quoted in Myrdal 1944, p. 22.
2 Hofstadter 1948, p. 24.

are as clearcut as the cases of Patrick Henry or Thomas Jefferson. Sometimes people are not at all sure what the right principles really are; or sometimes they are not at all sure how those principles apply in the particular situations confronting them. So sometimes getting people to *do* what is morally correct involves the more familiar task of getting them to *see* what is morally correct, in the first place.

That task, of course, is the traditional province of moral philosophy. Even there, though, the emphasis and tone of the two projects – of motivating moral behavior, as opposed to merely revealing morality's requirements – differ dramatically. Ordinarily, the proofs of moral philosophers are pretty well finished once moral truth has been revealed.[3] By and large, discussions of how to motivate moral behavior start where those other discussions leave off. They ask how we can get people to do the right thing, once its rightness has been demonstrated conclusively.

In this, I shall merely be respecting what has been dubbed "Hume's axiom": the proposition that, "Only motivations motivate." Suppose someone has acted so as to further a collectively desirable outcome. "His so acting cannot be explained merely by the fact that it furthers that outcome, or merely by his knowing that it does," this axiom would hold; instead "his so doing must be explained by some disposition or desire that he [actually] has." From this same basic axiom it follows, furthermore, that "if one wants people to pursue such outcomes, one will have to see that appropriate motivations do actually exist to produce that result."[4] Merely moralizing about the matter will not, in and of itself, necessarily suffice to move people.

---

3 Motivational issues enter into ordinary moral philosophy mainly as mere constraints: if people do not have it within them to act on those ideals, then there is no point (some would say that there is no sense, even) in advocating them as ideals. As Nagel (1989, pp. 903–4) puts it, "Political theory . . . has both an ideal and a persuasive function. It presents an ideal of collective life, and it tries to show people one by one that they should want to live under it. These ambitions may . . . necessarily interfere with one another. An ideal, however attractive it may be to contemplate, is utopian if real individuals cannot be motivated to live by it. But a political system that is completely tied down to individual motives may fail to embody any ideal at all." See similarly Urmson 1958 and Nagel 1970.

4 Williams 1988, p. 9. See similarly the analysis of "weakness of will" offered by Davidson (1969) and Elster (1984, esp. chap. 2).

That motivational task might still be a philosophical one, at least in part. But it is also a sociological and political one. In understanding why people do not always do what morally they should, and how we can somehow make them do better, it simply does not pay to be overly respectful of artificial scholarly boundaries. All too often, those tend to parse what is, from the agent's own point of view, a single set of tolerably well-integrated phenomena. In what follows, therefore, I shall alternate – with little warning and few apologies – between philosophy, law, political science, economics, and sociology, following the argument wherever it naturally leads.

There are many very different kinds of questions to be raised about morals and motives. My own interest in the matter is easily misunderstood, since the most standard reason (within moral philosophy, anyway) for taking an interest in these matters is not in fact my own. It is best, therefore, to explain at the outset the differences between mine and other more standard approaches to these topics, in order to forestall possible misunderstandings.

The problem arises principally because there is one school of philosophers, to which I do not subscribe, for whom questions of motive and intention lie at the very core of moral assessment. For philosophers of this persuasion, acting from the right motive is the very essence of morality. Neither acts nor their outcomes are good or bad, right or wrong, in and of themselves. Everything, they would say, depends upon the intentions and motives with which the acts were performed.

On this account, for example, sending food to drought-stricken Somalia is not necessarily morally good. We may be doing so merely to clear domestic commodity markets; and if that is our motive, then it is an ignoble act regardless of how many people are saved from starvation by the food that we send.[5] Neither, on this account, is killing necessarily morally evil. Our motive in bombing Hiroshima might have been merely to end the war sooner. If so, then that laudable motive

5 Saylor 1977, p. 202; Destler 1978. See similarly Hayter 1981 on the Brandt commission's motives in recommending more foreign aid from the First World to the Third.

might suffice, morally, to salvage an act that resulted in horrible deaths for countless innocent civilians.[6]

Were we to assess actions according to motives rather than outcomes, then acts that look right on the grounds of their good effects might easily turn out to be very wrong, and vice versa. By the same logic, we may well be led to punish evil motives that are of utterly no consequence. *In extremis*, we may even be led to endorse the suggestion of the seventeenth-century English jurist and wit, John Selden, that witchcraft should indeed be punishable by death – not because purported witches actually harm anyone, but merely because of the malice manifested by anyone attempting to bewitch another.[7] It is the evil of the sheer motives, rather than any conceivable effects that those acts might have, that Selden and his camp would have us punish.[8]

Moralists worried about people's motives for their actions are, most commonly, worried on just those grounds. They think that the moral quality of the act itself is determined by the moral quality of the motives from which it proceeds. They feel themselves incapable of passing moral judgment on what people have done until they know why they did it.

Unlike those writers, I do not suppose that motives are somehow constitutive of moral rightness in any such way. To my way of thinking, sending food to the starving is good, because of its good consequences, quite regardless of our motives in sending it.[9] By the same token, I do not think that

6   Anscombe 1965 floats this proposal, although in the end even she is not prepared to press the doctrine of "double effect" that far.

7   As Selden (1689) says in the entry under "Witches" in his delightful collection, *Table Talk*: "If one should profess that by turning his Hat thrice and crying Buz, he could take away a Man's life, though in truth he could do no such thing, yet [it] were a just law made by the state, that whosoever should turn his Hat thrice, and cry Buz, with an intention to take away a Man's Life, shall be put to death. . . . The Law against Witches does not prove there be any [witches]; but it punishes the Malice of those People, that use such means to [attempt to] take away Men's Lives."

8   An alternative – and more sensibly consequentialistic – reading would have it that Selden wants to punish the wickedness of merely trying to *frighten* other people.

9   The contrast between motives and outcomes does not capture all options in the dispute between deontologists and consequentialists, of course. Deontologists may, for example, trace the rightness of an act to the "character" of that action, defined somehow in terms independently of

the evil of killing innocent people is wholly erased simply by saying that it was merely a by-product – clearly foreseen, but entirely unintended – of something else that we were trying to do.

By all means, I would say, let us punish even unsuccessful attempts to commit criminally injurious acts against others. But let us do so not on the grounds of the mere malice that they manifest. Let us do so, instead, on the grounds that attempted criminality sometimes succeeds, and the best way of deterring attempts destined to succeed is to deter attempted criminality *tout court*. By all means let us reward people for acting from good motives. But, again, let us do so on the grounds that good motives characteristically carry good consequences, rather than on account of any excellence of the motives, in and of itself.[10]

A s it happens, most actions – both individual and particularly collective ones – probably proceed from a multiplicity of motives, some good and some bad, anyway. Furthermore, there is ordinarily no reason for people to try to pin down their own real motives too closely; indeed, on the contrary, ordinarily there is actually some good reason for them not to do so.[11] So in a way it does not really even make very much sense to expect a conclusive answer to the question, "What motive lay behind that act?"

Even if the question did admit of a conclusive answer, though, I am not persuaded that anything morally important would follow from it. My own definition of good and bad acts

---

the agent in performing it: it is an instantiation of the principle of "telling the truth," or whatever. Those are larger issues that, strictly speaking, lie beyond the bounds of the present project. In what follows, I shall be taking a starkly consequentialistic line which is therefore only partially argued for in what I have said here.

10 Adams 1976.
11 Goodin 1989. Godwin (1798, bk 2 chap. 4) similarly argued: "In the same manner as the grounds of our opinions are complicated, so are the motives to our actions. It is probable that no wrong action is perpetrated from motives entirely pure. It is probable that conscientious assassins and persecutors, have some mixture of ambition or the love of fame, and some feelings of animosity and ill will. But the deception they put upon themselves may nevertheless be complete. They stand acquitted at the bar of their own examination. . . ."

would turn entirely upon the good and bad consequences that those acts have, and not at all on any analysis of the motives lying behind them. I would be perfectly content to get people to perform good acts and to abstain from bad ones for whatever motives we can. Doing the right thing for the wrong reason is fine by me – or, anyway, I do not think that doing it for the wrong reason in any way undermines the rightness of the action.[12]

Sometimes we can indeed get people to do good things for dubious reasons. When we can, there is to my way of thinking no moral reason why we should not pursue that option.[13] Shipments of American grain to the starving in the Third World is promoted, in part, by a desire to offload surpluses that are costly to store. No matter. Foreign economic assistance from the First World to the Third is prompted, in part, by a desire to stimulate demand for First World products abroad. Again, no matter. President Lincoln's abolitionist mandate in the 1860 American election was born partly out of a genuine concern among white voters with the plight of the black but partly, also, out of a selfish concern among whites that there would be less of a market for free labor if the system of slave labor should spread any further.[14] Again, no matter. In all

12　The "deterrent" aspect of the criminal law is a case in point. What we are most concerned to ensure is that people abide by the law. It might be nice if they did so for the right reasons (because they wanted to, because they were considerate of the interests of others, and so on). But it is enough that they do so because they fear the consequences of doing otherwise. Information about people's motives – *mens rea* – may be required to prove that people have behaved wrongly. But no such evidence of good will is required for us to conclude that they have behaved properly: it is enough that they have behaved correctly, whatever their motive; whether it be love of their neighbor or fear of punishment simply does not matter.

13　There may, of course, be plenty of pragmatic reasons. Conspicuously among them might be the fact that my seeing you do good things for bad reasons leads me to do fewer good things myself, so on net less good is done if we encourage it to be done even for the wrong reasons. Richard Titmuss (1971) has famously argued that this is the case with the blood transfusion services: the more blood that is bought, the less that is given freely by volunteers. Elsewhere I have offered a range of examples to suggest that this may be much more than a marginal phenomenon (Goodin 1982, chap. 6).

14　Hofstadter 1948, p. 113. Recent econometric evidence seems to bear out their fears, at least in part: on large farms run on a "work gang" basis,

those cases, the right things get done, whatever the reason. And the fact that they are sometimes done for the wrong reason nowise compromises their rightness.

Still, I *am* in this book genuinely concerned with getting people to act from moral motives, to do the right thing for the right reason. My concern, though, is pragmatic rather than principled. I do not subscribe to the view that an act cannot be morally worthy unless motivated by worthy motives. But I do suppose that if we are going to secure morally desirable outcomes, then the best way of doing so – over the long haul, anyway – is by encouraging people to act on morally worthy motives.

The pragmatic point that I see as central is just this. We want to get people to do the right thing *regularly* and *systematically*; and the surest way to do that simply has to be to get them to do the right thing for the right reason. Certainly it is possible to rig the incentives in such a way as to induce people to do the right thing for wrong reasons, from time to time. But rig the incentive structure as we may, we can never make incentives track perfectly with moral rightness every time.[15]

Another way of putting the same point is this. Suppose that what makes the act right is one thing, and what makes people do it is quite another. If so, then there will inevitably be some room for slippage between the two. That scope for slippage would be absent, however, where people's actions were responding directly to the rightness of the act itself.

Of course, strategies for motivating moral behavior are as imperfect as any others. Hence we cannot realistically expect on all occasions to make people's actions respond, directly and perfectly, to the rightness of the act. In any particular case, it must therefore be an open question whether we would be more successful in producing the right moral results by appealing to the better side of people's personalities or to the worse. In any particular case, rigging the situation so that people who are acting from patently immoral motives would nonetheless produce morally desirable outcomes might be a surer strategy for securing those outcomes than would be trying to achieve

---

free and slave labor were complements rather than substitutes for one another; but on small farms without large work gangs, the two were indeed substitutes (Field 1988).

15   Nozick 1981, pp. 317–62.

the same results by necessarily imperfect appeals to people's moral principles.[16]

Exploring ways of rigging social incentives in such a way as to transform bad motives into good results is a project that is both intellectually interesting and politically important. Here, however, I prefer to concentrate instead on the other side of political life. I do so not because I think it is somehow more exalted to appeal to moral motives. Rather, I do so merely because I think there might be more chance of saying something general and systematic on that subject than the other.

The devious manipulation of evil intent to good effect is, I suspect, more an art than a craft. It calls for a creative, imaginative response to the peculiarities of circumstance. Appeals to moral motives might, in contrast, admit of a more formulistic, patterned approach. It is to this search for formula for evoking moral behavior in mass politics that the coming chapters will be devoted.

The classic question at the core of traditional moral philosophy is, "What course of action would be morally most worthy?" The question at the core of the present discussion is, "How can we get people to perform those actions?" The two projects are obviously related. Equally obviously, they are far from identical.

It might be supposed that the present project can get underway only after that other one has been completed. There is no point asking how to get people to do the right thing until you have a workable theory of morality telling you, and them, what would be the right thing for them to do. Furthermore, the one project may even be thought to render the other redundant. To some extent, simply showing people what the moral course of action is might sometimes suffice to induce them to pursue it.

There is much merit in that line of reasoning. Nonetheless, this book is not intended as an exercise in moral philosophy, strictly speaking. It is not my aim here to establish any novel substantive claims about what, exactly, morality requires of us. That is an important topic in its own right, and one on which I

16 In a way, this is just an application of the "general theory of second best"; see Lipsey and Lancaster 1956.

have certain views of my own.[17] But that is a large topic in its own right, and a quite separable one.

I trust that everything I say here is compatible with my own moral theories propounded elsewhere. But, by the same token, I trust that nothing said here depends in any way upon the finer points of the substantive moral views there propounded. There is no agreed first-order theory of morality, and I do not want what I have to say on questions of motivation to turn upon any possibly idiosyncratic conclusions of any particular first-order moral theory.

In raising questions about moral motivation independently of questions of first-order substantive morality in this way, I shall in certain respects be putting the cart before the horse. Even if only for purely expository purposes of illustrating my arguments, some first-order moral theory is needed to tell us what behavior would in fact be moral if we are to address questions of how to motivate people to behave in ways that count as "moral." And, of course, anyone wanting actually to implement any of the strategies that I shall here be recommending will need a still fuller first-order moral theory to do so.

Since my focus in this book is upon the motivation rather than the content of moral behavior, though, I really do want, insofar as possible, to take morality's requirements as read and to concentrate instead upon how to get people to act upon them. For those purposes, I shall therefore be seeking minimally contentious examples of acts that would be morally required from just about any perspective. I shall be seeking examples of bare-bones moral codes which can be pretty widely agreed to be valid, at least so far as they go. With some such first-order moral verdicts in hand, I shall then set about the task of seeing how we might secure compliance with the dictates of that minimal morality.

The Golden Rule, in its various guises, fills that minimalist bill admirably. Morally, the Golden Rule – "do unto others as you would have them do unto you" – is indeed the least common denominator. Certainly it is so at least among all extant Western moral codes, however diverse they otherwise might be. Occasionally, in what follows, a little more substance must be added to the sparse formal structure of Golden Rule

17 For elaboration, see Goodin 1985a.

morality in order to derive precise implications for particular sorts of cases. But I shall try, insofar as possible, to stick to that common moral ground for the moral judgments I will here be employing to raise the larger motivational questions that are actually at the core of my present concerns.

Many might scoff at the inadequacies of the Golden Rule, even as just a rough working definition of what morality requires. They might suspect that virtually any action can, with sufficient twisting and turning, be squared with that rule. That cynicism might be further fueled by the selfsame argument that I have just given for supposing that Golden Rule morality is a least-common-denominator morality in the first place. Precisely because the Golden Rule commits us to so little, it is consistent with almost anything we might care to do. And that would make it pretty useless as a moral touchstone, even for the minimal purposes here required.

But that argument badly underestimates the extent to which even a minimal moral code like the Golden Rule constrains people's ordinarily avaricious impulses. In effect, the Golden Rule rules out, in one fell swoop, all claims containing personal names and first-person pronouns as being *prima facie* immoral. Even if those morally disreputable claims can, with sufficient twisting and turning, be reintroduced in another guise, forcing people to twist and turn in these ways – to generalize and universalize their claims, applying them to a broader class of claimants beyond themselves and their immediate group – is an important step toward developing a genuinely moral consciousness. Even those who do not suppose that all of morality can be extracted from the bare, formalistic bones of the Golden Rule can generally agree that this is a very useful service, so far as it goes.

There is one case that is ordinarily thought to slip the net of Golden Rule morality. The spectre is that of the "moral fanatic," understood as someone who is prepared to universalize his pernicious principles even to his own great personal disadvantage. The standard example is that of the fanatical Nazi: when asked whether he would be prepared to be gassed himself, should he turn out to be a Jew, he agrees that he should be put into the gas chamber along with all the rest.[18]

18   Hare 1963, chap. 9.

That example might seem somewhat far-fetched. (After all, Hitler himself was always anxious to deny his Jewish ancestry; he never seemed willing to apply his own racial purity principles to himself.) But other real-life examples of such fanatical perversion of Golden Rule principles can surely be found.

Consider, in this connection, the argument put by the Minister for Bantu Administration and Development, in introducing into the South African House of Assembly the "Self-Government Bill" that created tribal homelands:

> The philosophy of life of the settled white population in South Africa . . . rests on three main basic principles. . . . The first is that God has given a divine task and calling to every people in the world, which dare not be . . . denied by anyone. The second is that every People in the world, of whatever race or color, just like every individual, has an inherent right to live and develop. . . . In the third place, it is our deep conviction that the personal and national ideals of every individual and of every ethnic group can best be developed within its own national community. . . . This is the philosophic basis of the policy of apartheid. . . . To our People this is not a mere abstraction which hangs in the air. It is a divine task which has to be implemented and fulfilled systematically.[19]

The Minister went on to add, pointedly, "We grant to the Bantu what we demand for ourselves. . . . If the white man is entitled to separate national existence, what right have we to deny that these peoples have a right to it also? Let us be honest and fair."[20]

The Afrikaner appeal to the Golden Rule ethic of universalizability might well be disingenuous, of course. The right way – the more challenging way – to put the question of universalization would, perhaps, be to ask if the Afrikaner would be prepared to go and live in the Bantu homeland if it turned out that his own true parentage was other than he believed it to be. That reformulation, perhaps, would force the Afrikaner to see that the principle he really wants to universalize is one that

---

19 M. D. C. de Wet Nel, in *Hansard*, 18 May 1959, col. 6023; quoted in Moodie 1975, p. 266.
20 Ibid.

holds that every people is entitled to an *equally good* homeland. And that, obviously, is something else altogether.

But we should not assume too readily that the dedicated Afrikaner would succumb to such treatment. For those deeply and genuinely committed to the notion of a People and all that goes with it, the reply might well come that the salient feature of the Bantu is that they are a traditional tribal people, and that their character as a people would somehow be contaminated or corrupted were they to enjoy a material standard of living akin to that of white South Africa. So one might well imagine a really sincere Afrikaner, committed to the flourishing of Peoples according to the divine will, honestly reporting that he would be prepared to go quietly to the homeland were the tables at the Registry of Births turned.

Insofar as agents are genuinely fanatical in that way about their moral principles, the mechanisms I shall here be proposing for evoking moral behavior will do little to quell their fanaticism. From the Afrikaner's point of view, apartheid implements a rule of simple reciprocity – doing as he would be done by, as the Minister himself explained before the House. From the Afrikaner's point of view, uncertainty would hold no horrors – if he turned out to be a Bantu, upon closer inspection of his family tree, then living on the homeland would be the right way for him to live his life. Even principles of non-exploitation might not get much of a grip on him, since the whole point of hiving off separate homelands is to create free-standing communities, neither of which is in any way dependent upon the other. And all of this can be – indeed, has been – defended publicly, in statements to parliament and elsewhere. Or so the hard-bitten Afrikaner fanatic would suppose.

To get a moral grip upon the genuinely fanatical, then, we will need a fuller moral code than the bare bones of Golden Rule morality provides. Perhaps we will also need a rather different set of political mechanisms to help that fuller moral code get a motivational grip upon such people.

Before we go too far down that track, however, perhaps we should pause to ask really just how much of a problem the fanatic actually poses. In polities where fanatics predominate – or even where they are present in substantial numbers – they pose genuinely hard problems, no doubt. Still, hard cases make bad law and even worse political theory. It would be unnecessary, and it may even be counterproductive, to set up a system of law and politics and morality to deal with the very special problems posed by fanatics where there are actually very few of them present.[21] To do so would be to make them more central to the organization of our social life than need be. Madmen, perhaps, are better marginalized – at least so long as there are few enough of them to be held at the margins.

All of that is just to say that the best strategy seems to be to concentrate on motivating moral behavior among those broadly amenable to such appeals, and not to worry overly much about how to motivate it among those least amenable. Intellectually, the latter might be the better puzzle. Politically, though, the former is the more important project. Politically, the name of the game is to form the most broadly-based coalition possible in support of morally worthy causes. What I shall be offering throughout this book are a few strategies by which that game might be played more successfully.

My interests in this book are indeed primarily political. That is not to say that personal morality is unimportant, or that individual acts of personal kindness do not really matter. Clearly, such things matter enormously. Some would say that morality almost wholly consists in them.[22]

Political morality probably matters less for good, but more for evil, than does personal morality.[23] Living the good life, politically, would leave us empty, if that were the whole of our moral existence. But living the good life, in a fully rounded moral sense, is impossible unless we have our social and political affairs in tolerably good moral order.

Within the political realm, I shall further confine my focus largely (though not exclusively) to questions of how to motivate moral behavior among the general public rather than among political leaders alone. In the language of social scientists, I am primarily concerned to motivate moral behavior among the "masses" rather than merely among "elites."

In part, that follows from my decision to focus upon political rather than personal morality in the first place. That is not to say that the personal rectitude of political elites is unimportant, or that official corruption is morally of no consequence. But

21 Goodin 1982, chap. 6.
22 Anscombe 1958.
23 Moore 1970.

rather too much is made of all this, I think, by those who would analyze political morality almost wholly in terms of it.[24]

Not all personal corruption taints the political process all that badly. As one historian has said of elections to the unreformed British House of Commons, "The venality was easily exaggerated. A freeman who insisted on being paid for his parliamentary vote was not necessarily putting it up for sale. The candidate whom he favoured could not have it for nothing; but in many cases the other side could not have had it at all."[25] Likewise, perhaps, the personal corruption of individual members of political elites might often (though certainly will not invariably) be of little larger political consequence.

A second, more conclusive reason for focusing upon mass rather than elite behavior – and a much more important one – is just that politically it matters far more, at least in the long run. In the short term, perhaps the situation is standardly reversed. But for better or for worse, an elite cannot resist mass political demands forever. In the long term, the latter are bound to prevail. As the American humorist Will Rogers reminded President Hoover in the midst of the Great Depression, "You let this country go hungry, and they are going to eat, no matter what happens to Budgets, Income Taxes or Wall Street values. Washington mustn't forget who rules when it comes to a showdown."[26]

Of course, the showdown does not come immediately. Even if mass opinion necessarily prevails in the long term, it crucially might matter in various respects just how long that "long term"actually is.[27] At the end of the day, however, the issue is always how to get the masses to come around. Strategies that count on inculcating moral behavior in political elites alone, without any attention whatsoever upon doing likewise among the masses, are for that reason probably fatally flawed.

Perhaps "profiles in courage"are not all that uncommon

24   Cf. Thompson 1987.
25   Brock 1973, p. 28. See similarly Scott 1972, chap. 2 and Heidenheimer 1970.
26   Quoted in Schlesinger 1957, vol. 1, p. 212.
27   If it is long enough, there may be time enough to count on inculcating moral behavior in political elites who, in turn, have time to bring the masses around to their way of thinking without having to pay the ultimate political price for their relatively greater moral enlightenment.

among politicians.[28] Still, it would be wrong for us to expect them, and more wrong still for us to count on them. It is purest folly to trust our salvation to a steady stream of saints and heroes, in politics as elsewhere.[29] And even political saints and heroes, prepared to sacrifice their own careers to some larger principle, will make no lasting difference to political life unless their example inspires others and, ultimately, the populace at large. It is, therefore, motivating moral behavior in mass politics rather than motivating elite behavior that will principally concern me here.

Beyond all that, there is a third and much more pragmatic reason for such a focus. Questions of how to motivate mass behavior simply admit of generalization in a way that questions of how to motivate particular persons in elite positions do not – or, anyway, not nearly so easily.

Elite behavior is not wholly idiosyncratic, of course. There may be certain sorts of interests and values that come with the job, forcing certain common concerns upon anyone occupying a position of power within society. And the ruling elite might itself be either sufficiently large or sufficiently homogeneous to allow us to make certain limited statistical generalizations about it as a whole.

Still, the "law of large numbers"is not going to help nearly as much in framing reliable general rules for evoking moral behavior from even moderately large elites as it will in dealing with the inevitably very much larger mass publics. In trying to evoke moral behavior from particular individuals in particular positions of power in any given society, we both can and must be far more sensitive to the peculiarities of the individuals involved. Generalizations of the sort that I am seeking here about how best to motivate moral behavior make sense only as applied to large groups and mass publics.[30]

28 Kennedy 1955.
29 Urmson 1958. While we cannot seriously expect heroic self-sacrifices from politicians, we can nonetheless expect that at least they not "put moral considerations into abeyance" for certain purposes, in a way that it may be morally permissible for agents without any such institutional roles and duties occasionally to do.
30 There is, of course, a long tradition – running from Machiavelli to Pareto, Mosca, and Michels – according to which reliable generalizations can be made about elites on the basis of psychological drives and personality types. (For surveys see Bachrach 1967 and Parry 1969.) But even if that

For these quite separate reasons, then, I think I am justified in further narrowing my political focus largely to motivating morality in mass political behavior. It arguably matters more, at least in the long run; and there is more we can hope to say, in general terms, about it.

With these introductory remarks in place, let us now turn to the main tasks of this book. In exploring how best to motivate moral behavior in politics, I shall pursue two tacks. One is more moralistic in its basic orientation, the other more political. Each contains elements of the other, of course. After all, the aim in both cases is motivating behavior that is moral, and doing so in the political realm. Still, the emphases within the two tacks are distinctively different.

In the one case, the inspiration is derived from the language and literature of moral philosophy. Key notions there are ones like reciprocity, impartiality, and non-exploitation. In the other case, the the focus is more firmly fixed on more explicitly political mechanisms. Discussion there centers around things like extending the franchise, entrenching rights in constitutional law, and holding people accountable to public scrutiny.

It turns out that these are, to a very large extent, parallel conversations. Juxtaposing them in this way usefully serves two functions. First, of course, it helps us to recognize common strengths and common weaknesses within each pair of parallel strategies. Beyond that, though, considerable confidence in our results comes from converging on broadly the same conclusions from two apparently quite distinct starting points.

---

is so, elite choices are more sensitive to the circumstances in which they act and those circumstances are less standard than those facing masses. All that seems to suggest that mass behavior would still be more amenable to generalization, even if the Machiavelli et al. psychological speculation about elites is true.

PART I
The Moral Tack

TWO

Reciprocity and the Duty of Fair Play

In discussing how to motivate people to comply with the dictates of the moral code, understood in basically Golden Rule terms, I shall proceed from the easiest cases to the hardest. The first set of examples to be discussed is the least problematic, in various respects. These are examples of simple reciprocity: doing to others precisely as they have done unto you, and vice versa.

Pure reciprocity represents the most direct and uncontroversial application of the Golden Rule standard.[1] There is minimal room for interpretation or dispute as to what you are supposed to do when you are doing *literally* exactly the same thing to some other person as that person has previously done to you.[2] And if others will indeed do exactly the same to you as you have done to them, then the motivation for your doing unto others as you would be done by them is also perfectly straightforward. In a world of tit-for-tat retaliators, you do unto others as you would have them do unto you because they will do unto you precisely as you have done

1 Gouldner 1960. Barry 1979. Becker 1986.
2 There is still some room for interpretation, insofar as by "the same" we mean that you are to choose your action with the same intentions as – Davidson's (1963) terms, "under the same description as" – the other person has chosen his. Even the trade of commodities of the ordinary economic sort is complicated in these ways, when the commodities involved are defined discursively rather than ostensively (Bachrach 1990).

unto them.[3] The standard modern example is arms racing: the USSR acquires ICBMs because the US has them; the US gets rid of intermediate-range nuclear forces because the USSR gets rid of them.[4] For a more colorfully quaint example, consider the intermittent trade wars between England and the Hanseatic League in the late Middle Ages, characterized as they were by retaliation and counterretaliation every time either tried to gain a competitive edge on the other.[5]

Or for a more down-to-earth, personal example, consider the subway at rush hour. Garrison Keillor – a self-styled typical Midwesterner for whom "a comfortable conversational distance is about four feet" – remarks upon subway manners in the following terms.

> When people are squeezed tight, they become extremely courteous. No eye contact. No sudden moves. Nothing sudden. Nothing loud or rude. Ten of us stand in 12 square feet at the end of the car, 10 people carefully balanced as the train starts, 10 arms holding onto a bar so we don't lurch into each other, 10 people trying to maintain a half- inch space between each other.

And the analysis Keillor offers of this phenomenon is precisely that which models of reciprocity would suggest:

> It occurs to me, riding the subway, that the Golden Rule is a matter of great practicality, reminding you to look at every situation from both sides because the person you are doing it to today can do it to you tomorrow. Count on it.[6]

In all those cases, the reason one person does unto others as he would have others do unto him is relatively straightforward: they will.

In many respects, though, this straightforwardness is illusory. Simple reciprocity is less controversial than it should be – whether as a standard of fairness, or even as an appropriate

3 Axelrod 1984. Taylor 1987.
4 Brams 1985. Etzioni 1967.
5 Conybeare 1986, pp. 152–58.
6 Keillor 1991.

operationalization of the Golden Rule. "Doing unto others as they have done unto you" is hardly fair when it entails grossly differential benefits or burdens among the parties. An eye for an eye is hardly fair when one relies far more heavily on eyesight in his work than the other. A beer for a beer is hardly fair when the person who bought the last round is far richer than the one obliged by that rule to buy the next.

The story of this chapter, in a nutshell, is about how the simplicity of this model of pure reciprocity breaks down, under twin pressures. There are pressures of diverse tastes and resources, on the one hand, and of imperfect implementation, on the other. The combination carries important consequences for both sides of the moral equation. It becomes increasingly unclear what, exactly, morality-as-reciprocity requires. More importantly for present purposes, it becomes increasingly unclear how to enforce its requirements, once we have discovered them.

The political tricks to be addressed at the end of this chapter are, therefore, actually pretty good tricks. They offer invaluable solutions to genuinely hard problems of how to motivate moral behavior, understood simply in Golden Rule terms.

The basic moral notion at work in models of reciprocity is just that of elemental fairness. In its more attractive, positive aspect, the norm is just this: if others have incurred costs in order to produce benefits for you, it is only fair that you should be prepared to do likewise, come your turn. You should, in all fairness, be prepared to reciprocate and to incur similar costs in order to produce similar benefits for those who have borne costs to benefit you.[7]

Putting the point in terms of "taking turns" is presumably what leads some commentators to draw analogies to the rules of "games" here. Rawls, for example, calls this a duty of "fair play."[8] But it is more than a game. There is nothing necessarily playful in such practices. Much serious business is organized along precisely these lines.

Indeed, the entire market economy is organized around

---

7 This standard of fairness has been urged, variously, by: Broad 1916, p. 390; Hart 1955, p. 185; Rawls 1958, p. 178; 1967, pp. 9–10; 1971, pp. 111–14.
8 Rawls 1967, pp. 9–10; see also Rawls 1971, pp. 111–4.

some such principles. The whole point of economic exchange is that one cannot get something for nothing: each of us must be prepared to give as well as to take. Moral motivation need not come into it, by and large. That rudimentary norm of fairness is guaranteed by the legal structure undergirding the market itself – laws of contracts and of torts.

At one step back, though, those laws themselves are mere reflections of deeper moral codes. To make exchange feasible, we must make theft unfeasible; we must stop people from simply taking what they want, if they are to be given any reason to pay or to trade for it. But a preference for one way of doing business rather than the other – for a system of voluntary exchange rather than coercion and theft – is essentially an expression of a choice between alternative moral codes. That choice is deeply informed by considerations of prudence, of course. Nonetheless, when enacting and enforcing, by law, the rudimentary norms of fairness that make markets possible at all, we are expressing and acting upon fundamentally moral judgments.

Once those norms and enforcement mechanisms to ensure respect for them are in place, the market proceeds about its business without further recourse to ethical norms of fairness, so long as all commodities involved in the transaction can be exchanged simultaneously. In a barter economy, that is precisely what happens. Neither party needs trust the other; each gives and gets in return at one and the same moment. In more sophisticated economies, though, deferred performance on one side or the other is not the exception but the rule. One party to the exchange performs now, in the hope and in the expectation that the other will perform later, as agreed. At that point, some further recourse to ethical norms of fairness is required to underwrite the market once more: people must be morally obliged to keep their agreements, even when all their gains are in the past and all their costs are in the future.

In small, stable societies, where reputations are known and acted upon, those norms of fairness might once again be self-enforcing. After all, it is in no one's interest to deal trustingly with someone known to renege on agreements. In larger and more fluid societies, where one's reputation is not known and there are fewer on-going relationships, contract law takes the place of these more informal social sanctions.[9] The essence of

9   Goodin 1976, chap. 5. Taylor 1982, chap. 2; 1987, chap. 7.

contract law is to enforce fairness across time, ensuring that I will perform later if you perform now.

It is worth emphasizing, here, that it is of as much benefit for me to be able to bind myself, by signing a contract, as it is for me to be able to get others to bind themselves in this way. Odd though it seems, it is actually in my interests to be able to put myself in a position to be sued.[10] Here is why. Suppose you do not know whether I can be trusted – perhaps I am a newcomer, or perhaps we live in a large community and you do not know my reputation for sure. Then, in the absence of some external guarantee, it would be imprudent of you to enter into any dealings with me that involved deferred performance on my part.[11] Supposing that such a deal would benefit both of us, we both are losers. Being able to give you an ironclad guarantee that I will perform – by signing an enforceable contract, for example – is in that situation of as much benefit to me as to you.[12]

Hence, people's motivation in assenting to the rudimentary norms of fairness that are embodied in the ground rules of the market economy – laws of property and of contract – is by and large unproblematic. Of course in certain areas we would prefer that everyone else were bound by rules from which we are ourselves exempt. But we all, or virtually all, appreciate that that option is not a viable one.[13] Suppose rules really do have to apply uniformly, to all or to none, then we would prefer to have everyone, ourselves included, bound by those rules than to have none bound by them.[14] And that is enough

10   Schelling 1960, p. 43. Hardin 1982, p. 260.
11   There are, in fact, formal proofs that an incumbent's reputation acts as a barrier to the entry of new players in such situations; see Kreps and Wilson 1982, Milgrom and Roberts 1982 and Fudenberg and Kreps 1989.
12   Perhaps this can even happen absent "external guarantees" of the sort standardly provided by the "sword of Sovereign." Consider the way in which medieval traders respected the verdicts of private judges operating under the informal Law Merchant that governed international trade fairs in the late Middle Ages (Berman 1983, chap. 11). Their motive for doing so, of course, was simply to avoid the reputation of being an unreliable trader and loss of business that the such a reputation would entail (Milgrom, North, and Weingast 1990).
13   In certain areas (e.g., contract law, on the argument just given) it is not even a desirable one.
14   Hume 1739, bk 3, pt 2, sect. 2. Goodin 1976, chaps 4 and 5.

to underwrite, motivationally, the rudimentary fairness of the form embodied in markets.

Notice, however, that we have already moved some distance from simple models of straight reciprocity. It is no longer a matter of literally "doing unto others as they have done unto you" in the most straightforward sense of an eye for an eye and a beer for a beer. The essence of market exchange is precisely that each trades something that he or she likes less for something that he or she likes more. If what you get in trade is exactly the same sort of thing as you give, then there would be no "gains from trade." That is what is so pathetic (economically, at least) about the old story of the fisherwives being reduced to taking in each other's laundry: the pay that one gets for doing her neighbor's laundry she herself pays the neighbor for doing hers; and neither of them is in any way ahead on the deal.[15]

In discussing the rules underwriting the market, such fairness as is involved must appeal to norms of reciprocity at another level of abstraction. It is not reciprocity, in the sense of giving and receiving the same sorts of things. Rather, it is reciprocating each other's adherence to the same basic rules of the market – rules of property and contract law, as just described. You have benefited from their sacrifices in adhering to those rules, and it is only fair that you should reciprocate in turn. This is a more abstract form of reciprocity than an eye for an eye and a beer for a beer, to be sure. But it is one that is motivationally almost as straightforward: the reason I trade rather than take, in my dealings with you, is that you trade rather than take in your dealings with me.

The real advantage of this more subtle form of rule-based reciprocity, in the context of economic markets, is that it (unlike more simple forms of reciprocity) is capable of dealing with differences in people's tastes and preferences and endow-

15   Not economically, at least. But paid and unpaid work may be different, both sociologically and psychologically. If paid work earns more respect than unpaid, then by putting their washing activities on an economic basis the fisherwives will have gained, if not economically, then at least in terms of self-respect and the respect of their community. They may even have gained economically, if the sociology of the household is such that having earned the money gives the woman more power to dictate how it should be spent than she would otherwise have over the disposition of household finance.

ments. In assessing fairness in the context of market exchanges, that is not just an advantage but a necessity: there would be no exchanges unless people were different in some of those respects.[16] What is an advantage in the context of markets turns out to be a liability in terms of politics, though, as we shall now see.

It is with that which falls outside markets that real problems arise. Situations of "market failure," and the political actions necessary to remedy it, pose problems of fairness that turn out to be far more intractable, both analytically and motivationally. Analytically, it is harder to discern precisely what "fairness-as-reciprocity" might there require. Motivationally, it is harder to see how to persuade people to do what morality, thus construed, would require of them.

Market failure, at least of the sort to be discussed here, is essentially a matter of what economists call "externalities." The basic idea is that there are certain benefits and burdens that people create for one another that fall, somehow, outside the economic relation and for which, therefore, people are not legally required to compensate one another. The role of the state, a classical welfare economist would tell us, lies merely in forcing people to "internalize" those externalities. That is to say, the role of the state is to enforce the rudimentary form of fairness found in the market, where the market itself cannot ensure it; the role of the state is to force people to pay for all the harm that they do, and to be paid for all the good that they do, for one another.[17]

That might be easier said than done, of course. In a world of unregulated externalities, each knows that he or she benefits from being able to shift certain external costs onto others; and, ideally, he or she would like to continue doing so. But that is sheer folly – akin to wishing that others had to trade, while you could simply take. Assuming that, realistically, the choice must be between internalizing all externalities or internalizing none, it is perfectly plausible that people would opt for the

16 Or, perhaps, in terms of their differential information, which for present purposes I propose to treat as just part of their "endowments."

17 Pigou 1932, pt 2, chap. 9. Baumol 1965. Strictly speaking, of course, all that matters is that people be made to face the right incentives at the margin.

former.[18] The same thought that underwrites, motivationally, the rudimentary fairness of the market also underwrites, motivationally, the rudimentary fairness of political interventions designed to correct market failures, in the form of ordinary economic externalities.

There is one crucial form of economic externality that proves more intractable to such logic, though. That is the sort known among economists, technically, as "public" (or "collective") goods.[19] These are traditionally said to be characterized by two features: non-excludability and non-competitive consumption. The latter condition says that the quantity and quality of the good available to you is unaffected by my consumption of it. (Your television picture does not blur when I turn on my set.) The former condition – the one that is of more interest here – says that the same good must be available to everyone in the group, if it is available to anyone in it. (A television signal cannot be beamed over the airwaves to your house without being beamed to all the neighboring houses as well.)

Non-excludability makes the provision of public goods through ordinary economic markets virtually impossible. Why should anyone voluntarily pay for something that, if others buy, will benefit him anyway?[20] Since everyone is thinking like that, though, no one actually pays; and goods that would actually benefit all consequently go unprovided (or anyway radically underprovided) through ordinary market interactions. Hence the need for political intervention, providing public goods through coercively collected tax revenues.

---

18 That might be because people are generally risk-averse, at least when it comes to high-stakes issues. (Why else would they buy insurance against house fires, even while taking a punt on the horse races?) Or it might be because even those who know that, even though they are net gainers in the current distribution of external costs and benefits, they cannot be sure how long that will continue nor of changing the rules once their own situation changes. More will be said of this uncertainty-based case for fairness in Chapter 3.

19 Samuelson 1954. Olson 1965.

20 Or, more precisely, why should he make a contribution to the provision of a good such that: (a) if enough others contribute he could enjoy anyway, without contributing anything himself; (b) if not enough others contribute will not be provided for any of them, even with his contribution; and (c) his own contribution is unlikely to make the crucial difference to the total contributions adding up to "just enough" to provide the good?

The motivation for people's supporting such schemes is, in broad outline, once again relatively unproblematic. Of course each of us would rather others pay their taxes, while ourselves escaping paying our own. But assuming that is not a viable option, each prefers that all (him- or herself included) be compelled to pay for public goods than that no one pay for them. In this way, mutual coercion can indeed be mutually agreed upon.[21]

What is problematic is not setting up such a scheme in broad outline, but rather deciding the particular composition of the bundle of public goods to be provided in this way. A further feature of public goods (actually, an important aspect of the non-excludability feature) is that the very same good must be provided for all if it is provided to any, where we are dealing with a genuinely public good. The very same lighthouse warns all ships alike of the rocks. The very same nuclear umbrella covers all residents of the United States.

Now, to say that the very same good is provided to all alike is not to say that all of them like that good equally much. Some ships might have on-board radar, and not need the lighthouse at all. Some Americans, pacifist out of principle or unilateralist out of prudence, despise the nuclear arsenal that others among them cherish. Much though citizens" tastes and preferences for public goods might vary within the community, though, the very same goods must be provided for them all: that is just in the nature of their being public goods in the first place.

The problem this poses is one of fairness. In the first instance, it is a problem of figuring out what system of cost-sharing fairness actually requires in these circumstances. In the second instance, it is a problem of figuring out how best to enforce its dictates.

First, then, what does fairness require in such circumstances?
In our initial formulation, the idea was that where others have sacrificed to produce benefits for you, it was only fair that you should make similar sacrifices to produce similar benefits for them. In a world of simple reciprocity and identical tastes, that meant that you should, in all fairness, do unto them precisely as they have done unto you – an eye for an eye and a

21 Schelling 1971. Goodin 1976, chaps 4 and 5. These arguments, of course, just echo Hume 1739, bk 3, pt 2, sect. 2.

beer for a beer. In a more complex world of diverse tastes and market relations, analogous standards of fairness require you to reciprocate not the goods but the act – to abide by the same basic rules of behavior as they have done in benefiting you. There too, though, the idea is that you should, in some sense or another, "do the same thing they have done for you," if you are to treat them fairly. The reason that that is thought to produce fairness, in turn, is that complying with the rules will presumably entail roughly similar benefits and burdens all around.

Fairness in the context of public goods is not all that much different, provided everyone in the community has roughly the same tastes and preferences for the public goods concerned. If we are all equally keen on national defense, for example, then submitting to conscription yourself, come your turn, is your fair repayment for my having submitted to conscription before you.[22] There, as in the market case, fair play is simply a matter of doing the same as others, in the sense of submitting to the same rules as they – making the same sacrifice, paying a similar levy, or what have you.

The problem in interpreting what fairness actually requires comes instead when some people value the public good more highly than others, but (because it is a public good) all must be provided with the same level of it. Then asking everyone simply to reciprocate each other's performances – submit to the same rule, make the same sacrifice – is patently unfair. To adapt Nozick's deliberately silly example, suppose everyone else at your holiday camp has taken a turn serving as announcer on a public address system that you could not help hearing but certainly did not enjoy: in fact, it has made your holiday a misery. Then the others can hardly appeal to norms of fairness to make you take your turn as announcer. True, you have listened to their broadcasts throughout the previous days; but you took no pleasure in them, and the fact that you were subjected to such torture in previous days provides no grounds for compounding the pain by making you go and do likewise now.[23]

22   Rawls 1967.
23   Nozick 1974, pp. 93–4. In Nozick's own telling of the tale, we are asked to suppose that, while you enjoyed the broadcasts, you did not enjoy them to be worth one day of your own time; and of course Nozick goes

The problem is hardly confined to philosophical fancy. Consider the case of the most famous civil disobedient of the early American Republic: Henry David Thoreau. The troops that Massachusetts had sent off to fight in the Mexican war had marched off in his name, among others. Unlike most of his fellow citizens, though, Thoreau regarded this as a source of shame rather than of pride, and he refused to pay taxes to support those troops. His objection was not to paying taxes as such. In explaining his actions, Thoreau made a point of emphasizing that "I have never declined to pay the highway tax," for example: he was "desirous of being a good neighbor," after all. His objection was merely to the impropriety of making him pay for "benefits" that he regarded as burdens on his conscience.[24]

Whether we want to let people take matters into their own hands in quite that way is another matter, perhaps. Still, some such arrangement is clearly what fairness would suggest in these circumstances. At the very least, it is clearly wrong to apply the ordinary standard of fairness – forcing everyone to make the same sacrifice, just because they will be provided with the same good – when some will enjoy that good far more than others.[25]

Fairness in such circumstances would require us to try to equalize the ratio of benefits and burdens borne by everyone across the whole community. The ordinary way of achieving that, in the case of private goods bought and sold in the market, is to allow people to consume varying quantities of a good, according to taste. That strategy is unavailable in the case of public goods, of course. There, the good provided must be the same (of the same character; in the same quantity) for everyone.[26]

---

on to protest at the idea that you should be compelled, without your prior consent, to participate, however much you had enjoyed others' broadcasts.

24 Thoreau 1848, p. 43.

25 The same is true, *mutatis mutandis*, where "doing the same thing" would entail a greater sacrifice for some than for others. I shall continue to phrase the point positively, but I always mean for that to cover both cases.

26 While the public good provided must be the same for everyone – in the sense of equally available to all – different people can sometimes choose to consume relatively more or less of the good, according to taste. If you

That leaves us with two distinct strategies for pursuing fairness in the context of diverse tastes for public goods. The first is simply an evasion: do not supply public goods at all, unless there is broad community-wide consensus on their value in the first place.[27] Analytically, there is some reason to suppose that the logic of electoral competition might drive parties to pare down their programs to "least common denominator" public goods in this way.[28] Historically, the first public goods to be provided by any given nation do indeed seem to be ones whose value can be most widely appreciated: Ministries of Foreign Affairs and of Justice, the first to be established, presumably do cater to just such common concerns.[29] Even public investment in basic infrastructure (roads, bridges, harbors, etc.) presumably benefits everyone, even if it benefits some people more than it does others.

If we were to stop with provision of those public goods upon which everyone can agree, though, the upshot would be that public expenditure would be too small – objectively, and even subjectively. In the same way that people can realize "gains from trade" in ordinary economic markets, so too might they be able to realize "gains from trade" in the political marketplace. Each might suppose himself better off trading his support for an expenditure program that benefits another for the other's support for a program that benefits him. Each might suppose that what he gives up, in the trade, is not nearly so important as what he gets in return. Therein lies the logic of "vote-trading" or "log-rolling."[30]

---

do not like public parks, you do not have to sit in them; if you do not like public education, you do not have to attend state schools, at least once you have reached the legal school-leaving age. Of course, not all public goods are subject to differential consumption in that way; and such differential consumption will not resolve all the problems of fairness associated with them. Problems of fairness might remain in, for example, apportioning the costs for the provision of public goods that are available to all but used by only a few.

27   Alternatively, we could simply decline to supply the goods in question *as* public goods. It is usually possible (if sometimes administratively difficult or economically costly) to supply things usually offered as public goods in a private-good format instead. (Margolis 1955.)

28   Downs 1960.

29   Rose 1976b.

30   Buchanan and Tullock 1962.

Whereas the first strategy works by reducing the number of public goods provided, eliminating those for which tastes are not uniform across the entire community, the second works by increasing them. Included in this larger package will be a great many public goods of fairly narrow appeal. But they are all necessary parts of the overall package. Funding your pet project is the cost that, in all fairness, I must pay in return for your funding my pet project.

(Of course, when confronting any list of actual government expenditures we can never be really all that sure of the fairness of the overall package. The ideal is that the ratio of benefits-to-burdens should be the same for everyone across the whole community. But over the years powerful political interests will undoubtedly manage to add benefits and reduce burdens for themselves. So there is, to be sure, room for a fair bit of readjustment of the overall mix, even within the norm of fairness itself. Let us leave those imperfections and adjustments to one side, however, in order to focus upon the central idea at work here.)

The basic idea is that you should, in fairness, be prepared to support a package of expenditures containing some things I want but that you do not, in exchange for my voting for some things that you want but I do not. The crucial point, however, is that all those elements form parts of an inseparable package.[31] It is simply unfair for you to pick all the raisins out of the pudding that we are supposed to share. The essence of fairness, there, is that you must not try to eliminate all my pet projects from the package while retaining all of yours in it. That would be unfair in much the same way as taking my goods without offering anything in return would be unfair in the context of ordinary market dealings.

In ordinary market dealings, there is minimal risk of that. Ordinarily I will not voluntarily agree to an unreciprocated transfer; and the force of law will be available to stop the transfer without my agreement. In political dealings, though, the risk is real. This follows from the very nature of the public goods that are to be provided there. Public goods, by their nature, cannot be provided by voluntary agreements; they

---

31 Wicksell 1896. Buchanan has made a career elaborating this basic model: Buchanan and Tullock 1962; Brennan and Buchanan 1980; Buchanan 1987.

must, by their nature, be provided through coercively-collected taxes.[32] And no rule yet discovered for reaching public decisions on questions of taxing and spending can uniquely guarantee that principles of fairness, in this elementary sense, will be respected.

Unanimity is the obvious analog, politically, to the rules of the market whereby each must agree to any transfers affecting his holdings. But it turns out to be too close an analog. It reinstates all the same problems that we had hoped to overcome in shifting from market to public provision in the first place.

The unaminity rule, in effect, gives each person a veto on public policies. The idea is that they should use that veto defensively, to block proposals that cost them more than they are worth to them.[33] The same veto can be used offensively as well as defensively, however.[34] Just as each person in the market would try to free-ride on others' voluntary contributions to public goods provision, so too would each person in the public sector try to use the veto given them by unanimity rules offensively, to extract a disproportionate share of the benefits of social cooperation for themselves. No public good is voluntarily provided in the market if everyone tries to free-ride and no one pays for it. So too is no public good politically provided if each person vetoes any proposal that does not give him or her the lion's share of benefits-net-of-burdens.

The upshot is that we cannot count upon any mechanical way of ensuring fairness in our public dealings. No simple rearrangement of voting rules will do the trick. We must instead seek more subtle ways of motivating respect for norms

32 Or so the classical analysis would seem to suggest. More recent work on supergames suggests that public goods can indeed be provided "voluntarily" in supergame equilibria of exactly the same form required to support private goods markets. Or at least that they can be provided as voluntarily as private goods in ordinary markets: in both cases, contributions are extracted through the use of threats that would in fact be carried out if those contributions were not forthcoming. Important though these variations on the story are for other purposes, the analysis of diverse methods of and problems with using reciprocity as a way of motivating moral behavior are better brought out by sticking to the more traditional version of the tale at this point.

33 Buchanan and Tullock 1962.

34 Lindahl 1960, pp. 12–13. Barry 1965, pp. 245–59.

of elemental fairness among a citizenry diverse in tastes and resources. It is to these tricks that we shall now, at long last, turn.

The problem of fairness in the context of public expenditures, recall, is just this. How do we ensure that everyone respects the integrity of the package? How do we ensure that people do not try to keep all the bits of the tax-expenditure package that benefit them at the cost of other people, while trying to jettison all the bits of the package that benefit others at cost to themselves?

The problem, motivationally, lies largely in getting them to see the package as a package – to appreciate that, in all fairness, they must take the rough with the smooth within it.[35] Of course, thoroughgoing egoists with no sense of justice or fair play at all will remain unimpressed with the demonstration. They will have no hesitation in breaking packages apart whenever they can do so to their benefit.

To impress them, we would need to show that they are wrong to think that they can get away with that. And there is indeed an argument to be mounted along those lines: after all, it is impossible to produce a stable majority for the division of a fixed sum of spoils that all value equally;[36] and the thought that they are as likely to be winners as losers in this shifting-majority game might produce enough uncertainty to give egoists pause in setting off down that track of breaking up the packages in the first place. That is the subject of the next chapter, though.

For the moment, let us focus instead upon the case of people

---

35 There are actually two senses of "packaging" at work here, which might be usefully disentangled. Some policies are packaged together out of logical necessity, others out of political necessity. Consider as an example of the first the case of a road-building program and the road tax required to pay for it: if we are operating in a system in which it is impossible (constitutionally, say) for the government to operate at a deficit, then it is logically impossible to spend money without raising it first; and the tax and expenditure programs must therefore form a "natural" package. Other policies are packaged together out of political necessity: your support for my hospital is the price I demand for my vote for your harbor. It is the latter, more than the former, to which notions of fairness-as-reciprocity attach. In the latter, it is merely a matter of "fairness" (whereas in the former it seems something more) that you should accept both halves of the package if you take either.

36 Riker 1962.

who do have, and are prepared to act upon, a general moral
sense of fairness-as-reciprocity. These are people who see – or
who can be shown, in terms they will appreciate – the
unfairness of breaking apart tax-expenditure packages, keeping what benefits them at the cost of others while eliminating
what benefits others at cost to themselves.

What these people need to be shown is that any given set of
public expenditure policies form such a package, in the first
place. If they do, then such people can see clearly enough that
they must, in all fairness, take or leave the package as a whole,
on an all-or-nothing basis. But if the policies cannot credibly
be represented as part of such a package, there is no reason in
fairness why they should take that attitude toward them.

The issue here – perceptually in the first instance, motivationally in the second – is one of the individuation of public
policy packages. Where does one package end and another
begin? Which programs can be seen as being all part of one
package? Which programs not benefiting me nonetheless
deserve my support, as part of a package containing other
programs that do benefit me? Which are part of some other
package altogether, or of none at all?

One way of answering this question – perhaps the right
way, in some deeper sense – is to say that everything that
government does should be regarded as part and parcel of one
big package. If on net you are better off with all that your
government does than you would be without any of it, then it
is only fair that you should support your government in
anything and everything that it does. That is the classically
Hobbesian way of putting the point; and it is a way that Rawls
came awfully close to endorsing, at one point.[37]

But on the face of it, that seems mad. Why, draft resisters
asked, should I support my government's jingoistic adventure
in Vietnam just because I think it does good work in building
hospitals and roads and sanitary sewers?[38] Social life – even

37 Rawls 1967.
38 One way to put the point might be in terms of the distinction between
    two types of "packaging" in note 35 above. It is not just a case pf there
    being no necessity, logically, for the government to fight in Vietnam in
    order to build sewers in Vicksburg. Neither, pacifists might say, is there
    any "political" necessity in it: no other segments of the population are
    so jingoistic (or so insensitive to the benefits of good sewers) as to set
    the price of their support for sewer-building the condition that the

that subset of it we know as "political life" – is just not that undifferentiated. Phenomenologically, we just do seem to see social life and political projects as falling into various separate and largely self-contained spheres.[39] That perception may be perfectly groundless, philosophically, of course. But the perception is none the less strong for being groundless. If we are to get a motivational grip on people, we must take due account of the way that (rightly or wrongly) they actually see the world around them.

Hence, the question of how to delineate policy packages is indeed a live one. Policies are, or are seen to be, part of various different packages. People might be persuaded that putting up with certain programs not to their advantage is the fair return for public support of other programs within the same package that do work to their advantage. But they need to be persuaded, first of all, that the programs really do belong in the same package.

Essentially, that is a matter of showing people that what others get from the package is somehow analogous to what they get from it themselves. It is the closeness of the analogy between their pet projects and yours that persuades you that the projects really are properly regarded as part and parcel of one larger program. For this reason, it is easy for American policymakers to regard "water policies," for example, as part of one big, inseparable whole. Watering the desert is analogous to draining the swamps. Building dams to supply water to parched areas is analogous to building levies to prevent floods. And so on.

The example of American water policies as constituting a single package is relatively straightforward. There are of course furious disputes, of the ordinary political kind, about the precise composition of policies within the larger package. But

---

government fight in Vietnam. It is therefore not an unfairness on pacifists' part to refuse to fight – they are not jettisoning from the policy package any component that was crucial in getting anyone else's support for the package as a whole. True, though that may be, that misconstrues the draft resisters' larger point (and the one I mean to be making with this example), though. That point is just that there is no reason to regard all these policies as part of a single larger package anyway. They are chalk and cheese. What does building roads and sewers and hospitals have to do with destroying Vietnam, anyway?

39   Walzer 1983.

squabble though they might over the details, there is widespread appreciation among all beneficiaries of those public works programs that, broadly speaking, they all stand or fall together. So while competing with one another for the favors of the Army Corps of Engineers or the Bureau of Reclamation, all involved rally around in support of those organizations when they come under periodic threat.[40]

The example to be considered next is far less straightforward, and requires a fair bit more elaboration. It concerns the question of how to motivate mass support for the welfare state – a question to which we shall be returning from time to time throughout this book. There are many ways this might be done. Here is one: persuade the better-off citizens, who never expect to need welfare state benefits, that their support for public welfare programs benefiting the poor is the price that they must, in all fairness, pay for the poor's support for programs benefiting them.[41]

As will be evident from what has just been said, the trick here – what makes this a matter of "fairness" understood as "reciprocity" or "fair return" – lies in showing that the programs benefiting the poor are part and parcel of the same larger package that contains programs that benefit the rich. Everyone gets something out of public expenditures, to be sure. But what does the rich person's using postage stamps have to do with the poor person's using Food Stamps? It looks like a matter of chalk and cheese, again.

To some extent, of course, rich and poor alike do indeed use welfare state services. Both draw the old age pension, or at least both can if they want. Both send their children to state-supported schools, or at least both can if they want. Both go to public hospitals, or at least both can if they want. All that is undeniably true. But it is all also largely irrelevant, because of course the poor use – and have to use – those services in a way

40 Maass 1951, esp. chap. 2. Ferejohn 1974.
41 I hasten to add that I do not suppose this the best way. (That, in my view, is the uncertainty-based argument to be developed in chapter 3.) The trick here in view is a good trick precisely because no one would have expected it to work – no one would have expected an argument that starts from premises of fairness-as-reciprocity to justify unilateral transfers of the sort ordinarily associated with welfare states.

that the rich do not.[42] So this most straightforward sort of reciprocity will not get us very far in motivating the rich to support the welfare state. It is not a simple matter of the rich providing for the poor the very same service that the poor have provided for the rich.

Still, an argument can be made that there are services used by the rich that are, if not the very same as, then at least closely analogous to, ones used by the poor. The rich man's public tax relief on mortgage-interest payments is closely analogous to the public subsidy involved in public housing for the poor, for example. Both are, in effect, expenditures of public monies to provide for the housing needs of people in the community.[43] Both can, therefore, be credibly presented as part of one and the same larger "public housing policy." The rich cannot, in fairness, begrudge the poor their council houses while continuing to receive their tax rebates on mortgage interest payments.

Let us follow out that line of thought a bit further, to see if we cannot further broaden the "package" and hence the support for welfare-like policies. My thought here is just this. It has always been regarded as a curiosity – a great defect – of American social welfare policy that there is, in the United States, no "child benefit" payable to all parents as a matter of right and without means-testing. (Of course, there are all sorts of means-tested benefits – most famously, Aid to Families with Dependent Children, AFDC – but they are something very different.) In virtually all other civilized and indeed semi-civilized countries of the world, there is a child benefit as a matter of right. In the developmental sequence of social welfare policy, it comes right after Workmen's Compensation as the second law typically enacted – before invalidity, sickness, and maternity benefits, and before unemployment compensation.[44] The US has long had those latter programs, but somehow skipped child benefits. What sense can we make of that?

Well the first thing to say is that, while the US does not have a child benefit as such, it does make generous provision for

---

42 That they have to – they have fewer options of "going private" – is clear. Whether or not they actually do is, perhaps, another matter. See: Le Grand 1982; Goodin, Le Grand, et al. 1987.
43 Titmuss 1958a. Le Grand 1982, chap. 5.
44 Cutright 1965. Atkinson and Hills 1989, pp. 16–33.

child-related costs in the tax code. First of all, there is an extra allowance granted to taxpayers for each extra child they have in the family, to be offset against earnings in figuring taxes due. Second is the perhaps more novel fact that child day-care costs are tax deductible.[45]

Of course, all of that is hugely unsatisfactory in all sorts of ways. First and foremost, a tax-based policy of this sort is of most use to people with earned incomes large enough to require them to pay taxes. It is of no use, in its American form anyway, to low-earning and non-earning families. (In principle, a "negative income tax" could be paid to people whose deductions exceeded their tax liability; in practice, though, the case for a negative income tax is effectively dead in America for the foreseeable future.) Furthermore, this tax-based policy is no substitute for a European-style child benefit, because it gets paid to different people within the household. It is the parent most directly responsible for caring for the child who typically collects the child benefit at the local post office, whereas it is the wage-earning parent who sees the benefit (in a pay-as-you-earn system of taxes being withheld from pay, at least) from larger tax credits.[46]

All of that said, however, I want to go on to say that there is a widely unrecognized advantage of a tax-based child benefit scheme of the American sort. The advantage is just this: it helps everyone, those who need the child benefit and those do not alike, to see clearly that social provision for children is analogous to other tax-subsidized social investments that clearly do benefit them all. Setting the program in the context of tax credit policies more generally makes the child benefit part of a larger package. It makes it clear that you cannot, in all fairness, cut my child benefit, while your oil depletion allowance remains the same. And that, in turn, helps insulate American-style child benefits from the swingeing cuts that have been made, in real terms, to child benefits in Britain, for example.[47]

45   Atkinson and Hills 1989, pp. 28–31.
46   Baldwin 1989, pp. 28–9. Atkinson and Hills 1989, pp. 23–31.
47   And from the even more swingeing cuts that have been made, within America, to means-tested AFDC payments: see Hanson 1987.

That is a long and winding and frankly speculative argument, though. Let us close this chapter with a brief discussion of a much more direct and straightforward attempt at invoking norms of fairness-as-reciprocity in recent political history. President Reagan's first speech to the Congress proposed astonishingly deep cuts in the US federal budget. The details of that plan do not matter much for present purposes. What matters more is the way in which the President and his advisers argued for it.

The key to the strategy, as the Secretary of the Treasury put it, was that "practically everybody's ox is being gored."[48] What Reagan attempted was, in essence, a "reverse log-roll": everybody gives up some pet project, on condition that everyone else do likewise; and in that way spending, and hence taxes, can be reduced for all.[49] The President's Council of Economic Advisers elaborated on that logic, saying:

> Many current programs provide benefits to special interest groups. These programs are inefficient in that the gains to the beneficiaries are generally less than the cost to the public as a whole. Nonetheless, . . . it is extremely difficult politically to reduce such programs one at a time, since the beneficiaries would then perceive their losses clearly and seek to regain them. The alternative, which this Administration adopted . . ., is to reduce a large number of programs simultaneously. If enough cuts in both spending and tax rates can be made simultaneously, most individuals may recognize that, while they may lose from cuts in a specific program, they gain enough from cuts in

48 Donald Regan, quoted in Gregg 1981, p. 332. On the crucial role of the rhetoric of "fairness" and "law-abidingness" in these debates, see further Tulis 1987, pp. 193–7 and, more generally, Stockman 1986. I follow these commentators in speaking as if perceived "fairness" is what was crucial to public acceptance of the Reagan tax reforms. But I take Jon Elster's point (private communication 1989) that it might just be the fact that those policies (like wage and price freezes, as well) simply strike blindly that makes people accept them. It is not that they are or are perceived to be "fair," necessarily; it is just that, unfair thought they may be, they are not *intended* to affect people differentially.

49 This is, I am told, a familiar strategy among budget-cutters in Holland, where it is known as "the cheese-slicer strategy."

other programs and in lower taxes to compensate for their losses.[50]

Of course, it is only to be expected that, even with that logic clearly on the table, "there will be some who will raise the familiar old cry, 'Don't touch my program – cut somewhere else'"; the President warned as much, in his initial speech to Congress.[51] But the game was not going to be played like that any longer, if Reagan had his way. The hope was that, so long as "everybody perceives that everybody's sacred cows are being cut . . . the parochial player will not be the norm."[52]

The strategy worked, too, at least for a while. Budget Director David Stockman recounts one illustrative tale of departmental representatives coming to him with a plea to restore funds cut from the Export-Import Bank's budget. "Who are the Bank's major beneficiaries?" Stockman asked in slightly dog-in-the-manger fashion. When finding Boeing Aircraft Corporation's name on the list, Stockman recalls going into "this demagogic tirade about how in the world can I cut food stamps and social services and . . . job [training] and you're going to tell me you can't give up one penny for Boeing? . . . I've got to take something out of Boeing's hide to make this look right," Stockman told the Commerce Secretary, and sent him packing.[53]

The appearance of fairness, of course, was always more than slightly illusory. With two of the biggest-ticket items – defense expenditures and old age pensions – both being politically off limits to budget-cutters, the cuts could hardly ever have lived up to the advance billing that they were going to "hit all programs equally" and to "be shared widely and fairly by different groups and the various regions of the country."[54]

Still, contrary to all the standing assumptions and expectations informing Washington politics, Reagan's budget cuts were politically very popular among the public at large, precisely because they were widely perceived to be fair in this way. A misperception, it might well have been. But it was one

50   Weidenbaum 1982, pp. 45–6.
51   Reagan 1981a, p. 363.
52   David Stockman, quoted in Greider 1981, p. 27.
53   Ibid. p. 22.
54   Gregg 1981, p. 332. Reagan 1981b, p. 485.

that was both widespread and highly persuasive among the public at large. And, although the President naturally did not get absolutely everything he hoped for, the budget cuts proved successful beyond anyone's wildest expectations in Congress, too.

One would like to be able to say that the one caused the other: that Reagan's first budget enjoyed the Congressional success that it did because the public perceived its fairness and forced Congress to support it in consequence. Alas, matters are never quite so simple. There are other factors to be entered into the equation explaining the easy passage of the budget cuts through the policy machine. One is that the proposals were in place well before permanent heads had been appointed for many of the biggest-spending departments. That made it easier to get Executive Branch agreement of the budget-cutting proposals in the first place.[55]

What eased their passage through Congress was the shooting of President Reagan at a crucial stage in the proceedings. His proposals were swept along on the massive groundswell of sympathy for him and his program that followed that failed assassination attempt. It would be wrong to conclude that the argument from fairness can be motivationally compelling only when made from the hospital stretcher. But, clearly, that helps. Logic alone might not be quite enough to move people to action in defense of fair causes.

55   Greider 1981. Gregg 1981, p. 333.

THREE

Uncertainty and Impartiality

This book is essentially about how we might make the elementary moral principles embodied in the Golden Rule ethic motivationally compelling for people, politically. Golden Rule morality is, at root, a matter of impartiality. To say that you ought to do unto others as you would have them do unto you is, most fundamentally, to say that you should accept that the self-same rules of conduct should apply to both of you alike. No one should get any special treatment. And that, in turn, is just to say that we ought to be impartial in all our social dealings.

Philosophers have devoted considerable effort to finding ways of helping people to see what, exactly, it might mean in practice to be impartial in that way. The latest in a very long line of proposals is John Rawls's idea that we should imagine ourselves choosing the basic rules to govern our society from behind a "veil of ignorance."[1] We are asked to imagine that we have forgotten who we are, what our social positions and particular preferences and plans in life are.

Having forgotten all that, you are supposed to ask yourself, "what institutions would I favor, then?" Assuming you really have succeeded in imagining yourself behind this "veil of ignorance" – putting out of your mind all particular facts about yourself, your position, and your preferences – your answer to this question must perforce be an impartial one. The reason

1 Rawls 1958; 1971.

it must be impartial is simply that you would have forgotten everything that would be required in order to stack the deck in your own favor.

Of course, for Rawls this is all just a mind game. It is just a matter of "let's pretend." There is no suggestion that we actually are behind a veil of ignorance. For Rawls, this is no more than a useful device for revealing exactly what the dictates of impartial morality would require of us. But that, in and of itself, does not provide any reason for supposing that people will act upon those principles. Rawls's demonstration gets no motivational grip upon people unless they are already motivationally predisposed to "do the right thing, whatever that might be" in the first place. For those who are – for those who harbor an inchoate "sense of justice," as Rawls supposes most of us in fact do[2] – then this vivid way of revealing the moral truth may indeed prove motivationally compelling. If so, however, it is merely because a predisposition was already there waiting, in our motivational structure, for the demonstration of moral truth to link up with. For people who lack that sort of predisposition, the Rawlsian argument about what they would choose from behind the "veil of ignorance" simply cannot move them to action.

This chapter is devoted to discussing various ways in which something very much like what Rawls was talking about might get a motivational grip even on people who lack any such predisposition to behave morally from the start. The basic idea, here, is that a "veil of uncertainty" might do much the same work, in the real world, as the "veil of ignorance" does in Rawls's game of "let's pretend."[3] Rawls's model enforces impartiality by asking us to imagine we do not know our particular positions. The uncertainty-based model enforces impartiality by pointing out that, in a world in flux, we actually do not know, with any confidence, what our positions will be in the not-so-distant future.

I t is not hard to see how uncertainty, if genuine and pervasive, might play much the same role in the real world as the "veil of ignorance" plays in Rawls's mental experiment. Suppose

2 Rawls 1963; 1971, sects 9 and 86.
3 The phrase is from Buchanan (1987, p. 1436). See further Goodin 1988b, pp. 58–61.

the uncertainty runs so deep that no one can be sure of his own future position. Then no one can afford blithely to ignore the plight of any other, saying, "I'm all right, Jack." The reason, quite simply, is that he has no grounds for supposing that he will not be in Jack's position, come tomorrow. And that thought, in turn, gives each of us a powerful motive for wanting to establish a precedent for taking care of people in precarious positions like that, for fear it might someday be us who are in them.

Take the limiting case of complete uncertainty. We have no more reason for supposing that we will find ourselves in any one position than in any other. In that case, simple prudence requires us to weight each prospect equally in making our decisions. In choosing what rules are to govern our society's future, we assign equal weight to the interests of those in each social position, because it is equally probable that we will actually find ourselves in each of those positions.[4] In that way, complete uncertainty gives rise to perfect impartiality.

This is merely to sketch the bare bones of the "equiprobability model of moral value judgements" developed by John Harsanyi over the course of the past quarter century.[5] It is important to emphasize, though, that – insofar as the uncertainty is genuine – people manifest an impartial concern for all alike not out of any moral motives but merely out of prudent concern for their own future interests.[6]

Uncertainty can in this way make egoists, who are naturally

4   This, in effect, is to endorse the "Laplace rule of insufficient reason," whose formal attributes seem to make it compellingly attractive at least so long as we can actually enumerate all the possible outcomes (Milnor 1954; cf. Rawls 1971, sect. 28). Even when we cannot enumerate all the options, to say we will focus exclusively on the worst possible outcome is an extreme solution for which Rawls has been roundly criticized (Arrow 1973; Musgrave 1974; Hare 1973). More plausibly, we would look at the best and worst possible outcomes, in some weighted fashion (Arrow and Hurwicz 1972; Barry 1973, p. 91).
5   Harsanyi 1953, pp. 434–5; 1955, p. 315; 1982, pp. 44–8. See similarly Buchanan and Tullock 1962, pp. 78–9.
6   This argument obviously presupposes that you have sufficient concern for your future self (and, connected to that, that you will not have to wait too long for the effects of the uncertainty to be felt) in order for uncertainty about your future to motivate you now. The parallel between concern for yourself in the future and for others in the present is developed, in a different way, to argue for broadly utilitarian conclusions in Sidgwick 1907, bk 4, chap. 2 and Nagel 1970.

inclined only to look out after their own good, into utilitarians concerned to maximize the well-being of everyone in society.[7] More to the present point, uncertainty can in this way make amoral people, concerned only with their own prospects, into dedicated practitioners of Golden Rule morality.[8]

The Social Darwinist, William Graham Sumner's singularly nasty little book on *What Social Classes Owe Each Other* does not make pleasant reading, in general. But one passage in particular deserves to be quoted in this connection, for it shows how even the very meanest of social philosophers can be persuaded by this sort of logic. Sumner says,

> Environed as we are by risks and perils, . . . no man of us is in a position to say, "I . . . am sure . . . I shall never need aid and sympathy." At the very best, one of us fails in one way and another in another. . . . [T]he man under [a falling] tree is the one of us who for the moment is smitten. It may be you to-morrow, and I the next day. It is the common frailty in the midst of a common peril which gives us a kind of solidarity of interest to rescue the one for whom the chances of life have turned out badly just now.[9]

In short, it is ever so much easier imagining yourself in the position of the other when there seems to be some very real prospect that, come tomorrow, you might be.

The transfers from those who are advantaged to those who are disadvantaged which would be licensed under this scheme ought be conceptualized, accordingly, not as benefactions in aid of the poor but rather as insurance of a sort which is of

7 As Edgeworth (1897, p. 120) puts it, "Of all principles of distribution which would afford [an individual] now a greater, now a smaller proportion of sum-total utility obtainable on each occasion, the principle that the collective utility should be on each occasion a maximum is most likely to afford the greatest utility in the long term to him individually." That is why Edgeworth supposes that, "In the long run of cases, the maximum sum-total utility corresponds to the maximum individual utility," so even an egoist should in practice be a utilitarian.

8 It does so, at least so long as people are not *too* myopic: that is to say, so long as they weigh future payoffs sufficiently strongly, relative to present ones, to be persuaded that the risk of something bad happening to them in the future is a good reason to pay for insurance today.

9 Sumner 1883, p. 158.

just as much benefit to those who are themselves rich, but perhaps only for the moment. They may look like morally-inspired acts of egalitarian redistribution. But appearances might be deceptive. When my fire-insurance premium goes to pay those whose house has just burned down, it does not necessarily betoken any altruistic sympathy on my part for their plight; more often, I pay the premium merely with a view to securing similar protection, should my house catch fire. If the motives of the advantaged in supporting transfer schemes are purely to buy insurance in an uncertain world, then there is nothing genuinely redistributive about the trans-fers at all: everyone benefits from the insurance coverage, whether or not they actually have to claim against their policies.[10] It is that shared interest in self-protection that induces everyone to contribute to the insurance scheme and to whatever transfers from the lucky to the unlucky are entailed by it.

All of this makes perfectly good sense if people genuinely are living under conditions of extreme uncertainty. It is clear enough how, if everyone is equally likely to occupy every position in society, they will be forced to weigh each prospect impartially in making their decisions; and in so doing, the better-off will be induced to agree to programs to aid those worse-off than themselves, not out of any noble motives but merely out of self-interested desires for insuring themselves against uncertain outcomes. But all of that makes sense only if people are genuinely uncertain, and only if that uncertainty is awfully deep and pervasive.

In practice, it often is not. Victorian social reformers were well aware of the argumentative advantages that would accure to their cause, if only they could somehow show that "the chances of poverty were equal" across all members of society. Then, "none could say that they lost while another gained by paying for" social welfare programs. Unfortunately, as those Victorian reformers saw all too clearly, people's chances "are not equal."[11] They remark bitterly upon "the enormous diffi-culty which a man of the upper classes finds in completely ruining himself even by vice, extravagance, and folly; whereas

10   Zeckhauser 1974.
11   Booth 1892, p. 201. See similarly: Harman 1975, pp. 12–13; Benn 1978.

there are plenty of honest people who in spite of economy and prudence can scarcely keep out of the workhouse."[12]

People usually do think that they have a pretty good idea of what the future holds for them. They ordinarily suppose that the future will be pretty much like the present and the recent past, for them. The poorest and most vulnerable members of society could be rather more aware of the way that their plans might be upset by random, unpredictable events. But at least the vast middle classes suppose that they have a pretty secure position. Uncertainty is not, for them, felt to be all that much of a problem.

The more uncertainty diminishes, the more impartiality – or this reason for being impartial, at least – diminishes with it. If you know that there is virtually no chance that you will find yourself in other people's position, you have virtually no reason (of this insurance-based sort, anyway) for taking their position into account in making your own choices. We are back to the Rawlsian mind game; and the only power that the argument can exert over you motivationally is by appealing to your innate sense of justice and fairness.[13]

Perhaps Victorian social reformers may have given up on this line of argument prematurely, though. Perhaps we can show people that uncertainty is much more widespread and pervasive than they sometimes suppose. This is clearly true in certain exceptional circumstances – total war and general depression are two examples discussed below.[14] But it is arguably true even in more ordinary daily life.

Insofar as uncertainties really do run considerably deeper than we ordinarily suppose, there is much more of a reason – based purely in the selfish logic of self-protection and

12 Leslie Stephen, quoted in Booth 1892, p. 201.
13 Harsanyi (1955, p. 315; 1982, pp. 44, 47) himself sees his equiprobability model in this light.
14 Flooding in the Low Countries is another example that arose in Dutch discussions of these arguments. But upon reflection I am persuaded that that case is of rather a different character. It is true that there, too, everyone on the same flood plain is equally at risk of flooding as is everyone else. But if the flood comes, it comes to all at once. The thought that risks are equal will not, there, ground quasi-redistributive transfers from those who might be struck by disaster tomorrow to those who are struck by it today.

insurance against life's risks – for following the dictates of impartial morality than we ordinarily suppose. People may or may not appreciate the fact, just yet. But it really will then just be a matter of bringing the facts about the true extent of uncertainties home to them, in a compelling manner. Politically, motivating moral behavior will then require nothing more than teaching people the odds that they are really facing.[15]

In what follows, I shall be focusing primarily upon more systematic sources of uncertainties that affect all more-or-less alike. It is only right that that should be the focus, for the name of the game is to find good uncertainty-based grounds for everyone to reflect impartially upon the plight of all. But before turning to that discussion, it is important to note that in searching for systematic sources of such uncertainties (of the sort that something might be said more generally) we might be missing something that is empirically equally important and that might be subjectively equally compelling.

The point here is simply that there is a great variety of idiosyncratic, quirky, almost accidental ways in which fortune might deal any particular person an especially cruel blow. Quirky though they may be, these disasters are nonetheless important to the particular individual who suffers them. And saying that they are quirky is merely to say that no two people are likely to come to grief in exactly the same way, which is consistent with everyone being equally at risk of some such disaster or another. We might all be courting disaster equally, even if the disaster, should it come, will come to each of us slightly differently. If the risk of disaster that we are all facing is indeed broadly the same, then on uncertainty-based logic we all have similar motives for setting up institutions to protect anyone whom disaster might strike.

Consider in this connection, then, the cautionary tale at the core of Tom Wolfe's *Bonfire of the Vanities*. A filthy rich Wall Street trader, who fancies himself a "Master of the Universe," uses his millions to insulate him from the horrors of the low-life of New York's slums. But a single wrong turn on the freeway one night suffices to bring him face-to-face with the

15 And teaching them to react rationally to them, perhaps we should add in light of evidence from social psychologists about irrational responses to risks (Kahneman, Slovic, and Tversky 1982).

South Bronx in all its sordid glory, sharing a jail cell with rats and rapists.[16]

The story is fictional, to be sure. But the fact that the novel topped the bestseller lists for so long itself shows how well the story resonates with American city-dwellers, nonetheless. They do not all expect to make the same wrong turn; they do not even all expect to come to grief by having their cars break down while driving through the ghetto. But they all sense, perhaps, the precariousness of the barriers that separate their privileged existence from that of the urban underclass.[17] Those barriers might break down, for any one of them, in any of so many different ways that all of them, in effect, have the same strong motive for reducing the disparities between rich and poor in the innercity.[18]

L et us turn, now, to some more systematic sources of uncertainty that might be capable of generating impartial regard for others that might then get institutionalized into the formal arrangements of our societies. For a first example, consider the uncertainty associated with total war.

History clearly shows that that uncertainty clearly can force a more impartial attitude upon people and yield politically important moral dividends in consequence.[19] Of course, no

16 Wolfe 1987.
17 Psychologically, people are inclined to blame such disasters on some "unusual" – and hence rare and presumably atypical – feature of the scenario, like taking a wrong turn or the car breaking down (Kahneman and Tversky 1979). Ordinarily we do not try to plan too carefully for rare and atypical events, perhaps; so that psychological attribution would lead people to pay less attention, not more, to all the various, improbable ways in which they might come to grief. That tendency can be reversed, however, if – as I suspect – life in the inner city is now such that the "unusual" has become usual and the "atypical" have come to be almost expected.
18 Riding the subway, Garrison Keillor (1991) supposes, is crucial in developing this mindset. There, white professionals are "packed in so close to black men and women" which serves to remind them that "situations are easily reversed" and encourages the thought within them that "the person you sack today is the person you'll need help from tomorrow, the man you put in prison today will someday be the warden". Such *non sequiturs* are, perhaps, psychologically inescapable in the claustrophobic conditions of the rush-hour subway.
19 War might also serve to force us to face up to our hypocrisies. It clearly had that effect on American racism. "Our very proclamations of what

one would actually recommend total war as a positive strategy for making people more moral. But even awful situations can have some agreeable side-effects. Such was arguably the case with Second World War. The point about total war is that everyone is involved, by definition – and, importantly for the uncertainty-based argument here in view, pretty much equally involved, in one way or another.

Perhaps the most telling illustration of this point is the impact of the Battle of Britain and the mass bombings associated with it. No Londoner, rich or poor, could be altogether confident that he or his property would be utterly immune to bomb damage. Neither, as the bombings spread (and, later, with the development of the highly erratic buzz bombs) could many other Britons. Richard Titmuss spoke with feeling when writing, in his distinguished contribution to the Official Civil History of the war, that "damage to homes and injuries to persons were not less likely among the rich than the poor": his own London home was itself bombed twice during the course of the war.[20]

Indiscriminate bombing led to pervasive uncertainty. That, in turn, led to everyone's coming to have an impartial regard for the plight of everyone. As Titmuss says, "The assistance provided by the Government to counter the hazards of war carried little social discrimination, and was offered [equally] to all groups in the community. The pooling of national resources and the sharing of risks were not always practicable nor always applied, but they were the guiding principles."[21] The development of the War Damage Insurance scheme was the most direct response to such uncertainties. But other social policies evolved in the same spirit. Titmuss, again, remarks that "the acceptance of [the] social discipline [involved in risk-sharing]

---

we are fighting for have rendered our own inequities self-evident" admitted the titular head of the Republican Party in a speech to the NAACP in 1942. "When we talk of freedom and opportunity for all nations the mocking paradoxes in our own society become so clear that they can no longer be ignored" (Wendell Wilkie, quoted in Myrdal 1944, p. 1069). Titmuss (1950; 1958b, pp. 82, 85) makes much the same point about British war aims and class inequalities; he draws particular attention to the famous editorial to that effect in *The Times* (London), 1 July 1940.

20   Titmuss 1950, p. 506. Gowing 1975, p. 406.
21   Titmuss 1950, pp. 506–7.

. . . made necessary by war, by preparations for war, and by the long-run consequences of war, must influence the aims and content of social policies not only during the war itself but in peacetime as well."[22]

Thus it is no accident that a great many important components of the British welfare state were put into place – either as on-going programs, or at least as firm plans for postwar reconstruction – during the war itself. The Beveridge report's promise of the welfare state to come is the most famous of these, of course.[23] More impressive, in a way, though is what happened in the midst of the war itself. In the dark days of 1940 and 1941 – hardly a time for extravagant innovation, one would have thought – we see all sorts of new programs being introduced. Among them were: programs of free school milk and subsidized school meals; immunization and other programs for promoting public health, along with expansion of hospital services; increased pensions; abolition of means-testing for social service payments; assistance to evacuees, and aid to those suffering damage to life, limb, or property as a result of the war; and transformation of the Unemployment Assistance Board into the Assistance Board, with an expanded clientele including pensioners and those suffering war damage.[24]

Like all good stories, this one bears many alternative interpretations. But at least one of them is that the expanded sense of shared insecurity and uncertainty forced a more impartial attitude upon everyone in the country. There was a political consensus for sharing arrangements when they could be seen as being potentially of use to everyone that there never would have been when they were clearly of use only to a predictable few.[25]

Much the same story might be told of the effects of a general economic depression. Of course, we can never be absolutely sure of our economic futures, even in apparently settled

22 Titmuss 1958b, p. 85.
23 Beveridge 1942.
24 Titmuss 1950. Dryzek and Goodin 1986, p. 12.
25 Dryzek and Goodin 1986; the cross-national data analyses reported there suggest, too, that the increase in postwar welfare state expenditures worldwide is best explained in terms of the extent of wartime uncertainties, country-by-country.

times. Our personal finances can always suffer severe setbacks that were utterly unanticipatable ahead of time; indeed, we are increasingly aware that the global economy can always collapse around us, at virtually a moment's notice. Still, in ordinary times most of us can pretty well predict where we will be, economically, from one year to the next. Secure in that knowledge, we can safely abandon agnostic impartiality in favor of an attitude more precisely tailored to further our own particular interests.

The onset of general economic depression changes all that. When the stock market really crashes, ultra-safe "blue chips" crash right along with more ordinary investments. Those who had previously felt secure in the knowledge that they had a sizeable nest egg saved up in the bank might, in a general depression, see it disappear as their bank itself goes bankrupt. Those who had been trusting to permanent posts in safe companies for a secure livelihood might, in a general depression, find that even safe companies fail. And so on.

That is just to say that no one can count on being immune to – or even substantially less at risk from – the effects of a general depression. That is not to say that everyone actually will, in the end, feel the effects equally. Clearly they will not. Some will be luckier than others. And it may well be true that even those among the rich who happen to be unlucky will, on average, nonetheless fare better than even the relatively lucky among the poor – at least in absolute terms. But absolute terms might not be what matter most to people. Even if the unlucky rich could pretty well count upon being better off, absolutely, than the lucky poor, they will nonetheless have suffered serious interruptions to their previous life plans due to the decline in their present economic positions relative to their previous ones. Arguably, it is that sort of continuity that matters most to people, striving to give coherence and meaning to their lives.[26]

Since no one can count, ahead of time, on being immune to severe interruptions to their lives in the face of general economic depression, everyone must have an impartial concern with policies to avert that outcome. At the very least, that means that everyone should show an impartial concern for macro-economic stabilization policies to prevent depression,

26   Goodin 1990b.

and with macro-economic policies designed to bring an economy out of depression once it is underway. But with a sufficiently large risk that any among us, wherever we started out, might fall on such very hard times as to need to draw unemployment benefit or move into public housing, broadly the same logic may well lead to widespread support not only for macro-economic stabilization policies but for social welfare policies of a more ordinary sort as well.[27]

The key to that argument, once again, is uncertainty. It is the uncertainty of whether or not you will yourself need to draw unemployment benefit that makes you support a generous program of unemployment compensation. That uncertainty is arguably very great indeed, at least at the outset of a general depression. When the general collapse begins, there is no way of telling where it will end, or what will be left standing when it does. In those circumstances, it is only prudent for people to have an impartial regard for the plight of employed and unemployed alike, for they might well find themselves in either state.[28]

---

27 Heclo 1981, p. 392. The great theme of Keynes (1937), of course, is that uncertainty was as much a cause as consequence of depression: it is the great uncertainty of the returns on capital investment, in the circumstances immediately preceding a depression, that induces investors to opt for the greater certainty of simply holding money in liquid forms instead; and that is what precipitates the collapse. Suppose we could show that the same thing that makes the return on investments uncertain also makes it uncertain where the effects of depression would be most heavily felt. Then the two uncertainties would indeed be connected, and we would have succeeded in demonstrating that the same thing that causes depressions also should make people more impartial in their response to them, favoring in consequence social relief to all in distress.

28 By the selfsame logic, once the depression has pretty well bottomed out, the uncertainty once again begins to recede. Those still in work, at that point, can largely count on staying in work. And as the veil of uncertainty is lifted, so too is the imperative to display impartial regard for the interests of employed and unemployed alike. Those who now know that they are unlikely to need to claim benefits, after all, no longer have any self-interested reason for supporting benefits for those who do. That is one way of explaining why the Thatcher Government was able to get by with an increasingly less generous unemployment compensation policy despite the fact that there are more people now in need of it; see Atkinson 1990.

That logic is brought home to people particularly forcefully with the onset of a general depression. But, crucially, it is at least arguably almost as applicable even in what we have come to regard as "settled" economic circumstances. That is the astonishing lesson taught us by the enormously important work done by Greg Duncan and his colleagues on the University of Michigan's Panel Study of Income Dynamics in the US.

These researchers re-interviewed the same 5,000 families every year over the course of the decade 1969 to 1978 in order to see how family economic fortunes fluctuated. In aggregate, there was not much change: about the same proportion of families fell into each income class from one year to the next; and that is just as previous studies would have led us to expect.

The great contribution of the Income Dynamics study was to show that, although the proportion of people in each income class was the same from year to year, different people fell into each of those classes in different years. At the individual level, flux – not stability – was the rule. The aggregate-level stability, so widely observed, is simply an illusion, caused by many people moving up at the same time as many others are moving down. Indeed, "fewer than one-half of the population remained in the same economic position" over the course of the decade studied. One-third had "dramatic" improvements in their economic position, and one-fifth "dramatic" declines in theirs.[29]

Furthermore, the Income Dynamics study showed – again surprisingly – that these fluctuations in economic fortune were not confined to "marginal" members of the workforce. It is not just young blacks and working wives whose fortunes fluctuated in these ways. As we would expect, white males were the most stable group of earners in the study. But even for them, the average year-to-year change in annual income was 25 percent; 40 percent of them saw their annual income fluctuate by more than 10 percent at least six years out of the ten; almost 60 percent of them had declines in their annual income at least four of those years.[30] And even among those white males, "no identifiable group – not the more educated, not union members, not even higher-income persons – seems

29   Duncan 1984, p. 3.
30   Ibid. p. 212.

to be immune from these changes in year-to-year income. There is no evidence," Duncan and his colleagues conclude, "that there are secure, protected niches in the economy. . . . . Variability rather than stability and regularity characterizes the working lives of most men" in America.[31]

These fluctuations in economic fortunes are so severe as to force surprisingly many people to rely upon welfare state services, from time to time. "Major unemployment" hit 29 percent of married men at least once in the decade, with another 22 percent being forced to change jobs involuntarily at least once; work loss due to illness affected 28 percent, and total disability struck 30 percent.[32] Once those sorts of statistics are on the table, it can hardly come as a surprise to learn that fully "one out of every four Americans lived in a household that received income from on of the major welfare programs at least once" over the course of the decade.[33] What is striking, though, is the fact that those who received welfare benefits one year more often than not did not have to continue receiving them for more than two years. People seem to rotate into and out of welfare programs fairly regularly, with only about 2 percent relying on welfare benefits for more than half their income for 80 or more percent of the time.[34] Welfare truly is a form of transitional assistance. Most people's lives truly are – as the title of the Income Dynamics study would have it – characterized by *Years of Poverty, Years of Plenty*, in turn.

Just to drive home the point, let me quote the conclusion of that study in full:

> No broad demographic group in our society appears immune from shocks to their usual standard of living, stocks resulting from rapidly changing economic or personal conditions. For men, the shock often comes in the form of an involuntary job loss; for married women, divorce or the death of the spouse is often the precipitating event. . . . Few people are immune to occasional economic misfortune, and when it strikes, welfare serves as a kind of insurance for them, providing temporary assistance

31 Ibid. p. 119.
32 Ibid. p. 27.
33 Ibid. p. 90.
34 Ibid. pp. 90, 75.

until they are able to regain their more customary levels of living. . . . These people are "digging out' following a disaster. Welfare assists them during that process and then, in time, is left behind.[35]

Strictly speaking, of course, Duncan's findings pertain only to the United States. Still, there is no reason to suppose that they are peculiar to the US. The precipitating events he mentions – involuntary job loss, incapacitating accident or illness, divorce or death of a spouse – are common events in all societies. So we may suppose that broadly the same pattern may well be revealed in similar studies elsewhere.

The reason for belaboring these statistics is simple. If it really is true that everyone is seriously at risk of needing welfare state services, then – on the uncertainty-begets-impartiality argument developed here – everyone should, for perfectly self-interested reasons, support the welfare state. They would be impartial in their concern for all, on that model, not out of any deeper moral motive but merely as a means of self-protection in an uncertain world. Welfare programs would be a matter of insurance, not of sympathy or altruism or morality.

Anyway, that is how people should be expected to react on the basis of the uncertainty logic here sketched. The simple fact of the matter, however, is that they do not; the increasingly successful attacks on the welfare state in recent years bear witness to that.[36] Why not? We can only speculate. Maybe they do not know the facts. The results of Duncan's Income Dynamics study came as a surprise even to professional social scientists, after all; and they are only now beginning to percolate through even the "quality" press in the US

Or perhaps the explanation is that people know, intuitively, the facts that Duncan reports but psychologically distance themselves from them. People have a well-documented range of wholly irrational ways of coping with information about risks they are running, conspicuous among them the thought that "it will never happen to me." (One favorite example is the survey asking Chicagoians, first, what proportion of the population would die if an atomic bomb were dropped downtown: 97 percent would be killed was the answer. Next they were

35   Ibid. p. 90. Duncan, Hill, and Hoffman 1988.
36   Hanson 1987. Block, Cloward, Ehrenreich, and Piven 1987. Griffith 1983.

asked what they themselves would be doing three days after the bomb fell: 90 percent said helping to clear up. Only 2 percent said they would themselves have been killed in the blast.[37]) Maybe people are just fooling themselves, in that way, into thinking that they do not need to fear precisely the same things they see happening to so many of those around them.

Still, if the Duncan Income Dynamics results are right, there is much more scope for motivating people to support the welfare state for purely self-interested reasons than we might have thought.[38] If uncertainty really is that widespread, then there are objectively good reasons for people taking the sort of impartial attitude that morality would recommend. Instituting programs that would care for any in need, for fear that tomorrow that might be me, would then make sense to everyone. It is just a matter of making people see the sense in it – to face the facts, and to feel their force psychologically. Political action, there, might well have an educative role.

In making people "feel their force psychologically," we ought attend particularly to the "heuristics and biases" that social psychologists have identified in judgments involving risk and uncertainty. Among the most important is the tendency for people to be particularly sensitive to risks which are

---

37   Goodin 1982, p. 143 and chap. 8 more generally. Kahneman, Slovic, and Tversky 1982.

38   Strictly speaking, that argument just shows people that they have a reason for wanting insurance – it does not show, necessarily, that it should be "social insurance" of the welfare state's sort, rather than privately organized. Further argument is needed on that point. The first thing to say, there, is that if the risks really are so widespread and universally shared as I suggest, then there is no reason for anyone to prefer private insurance coverage. That makes sense only if some people are known to be better-than-average risks, and can secure lower insurance premia from private companies risk-rating their policies on proper actuarial bases. The next thing to say is that private market provision of insurance presupposes various conditions that are absent in the cases that social insurance characteristically covers. Most notably, the risk each runs is not statistically independent of each other's risk, compromising the financial integrity of mutual insurance schemes; see Barr 1987, chap. 5 and Goodin 1988b, pp. 157–60. The final thing to say is that in private markets it is logically impossible to insure against becoming uninsurable; yet being forced to "go naked" (in the parlance of the insurance industry) precisely when you are most at risk of something bad happening to you is exactly what even a midly risk-averse agent would most want to avoid.

particularly vivid in their imaginations ("psychologically avail-abile," in the jargon). Studies show that people systematically overestimate the chances of dying in dramatic ways – by snakebite, for example – and correspondingly to underestimate the chances of dying in more boring, mundane ways.[39]

When trying to use the uncertainty dynamic to evoke impar-tial concern for all we ought to take those lessons to heart. In media campaigns in support of social welfare programs, for example, we ought to take particular care to dwell upon the case histories of particular people who are unemployed or impoverished. Those should be people whom others can recognize as "just like" themselves. And we should present their plight in vivid, memorable detail.

In such ways, the psychological dynamic that usually ena-bles people unjustifiably to discount risks and uncertainties can be made to work in the opposite direction. It can be manipulated to encourage people to give those risks and uncertainties their full due – and with them, to give fellow-citizens fallen on hard times their full due as well.

Manipulate risk perceptions as we might, though, there will still be some people left unprotected by this uncertainty-based logic. Even if people were completely clear-headed about the real risks that they were themselves running, life's uncer-tainties simply do not run so deeply as to force absolutely everyone to manifest an utterly impartial regard for the interests of absolutely everyone else in their society.

The problem is particularly acute with respect to people suffering multiple, overlapping, and mutually-reinforcing dis-advantages within our own societies. Consider the plight of black Americans. As Hochschild remarks, "inequalities of race, class and power cumulate, and their combination worsens the disparities created by each dimension alone."[40] There might be many reasons why those disadvantages prove to be mutually-reinforcing. Among them, though, is the utter improbability (verging on virtual impossibility) of the vast majority of the more powerful members of society – middle-class whites with connections – ever finding themselves in the position of those

39   Slovic, Fischhoff, and Lichtenstein 1980, pp. 466–7; see further Kahne-man, Slovic, and Tversky 1982, esp. chaps 1, 11–14.
40   Hochschild 1988, p. 159.

who are multiply disadvantaged. Their future is subject to some uncertainty along each of those dimensions of disadvantage, perhaps.[41] But they would rightly regard it as wildly improbable that disaster should strike them thrice. Knowing that might be at least part of reason that they fail to empathize with (or to support programs to alleviate the plight of) those suffering such multiple disadvantages.

Emphasizing life's uncertainties is a good way of forcing us to cut a fair, impartial bargain with those who might someday end up top of our own society. But it still gives no reason for us to cut a fair deal with those in other societies with whom we can confidently expect not to have to deal in future. It does not provide us with any reason for cutting a fair deal with those within our own society we can be pretty sure will never end up on top. (Blacks in the American South, at least during Bull Connor's lifetime, might be one example; Catholics in Ulster during our own might be another.[42]) Neither does that sort of logic provide us with any reason for respecting a past deal made with those in our own society who we can be pretty sure will never be on top again. (Christians in the Lebanon might be an example: that, the standard story goes, is precisely why there has not been an official census since 1932; it would have confirmed too dramatically the Christians' demographic inferiority, once and for all.[43])

People in those sorts of position are, in terms of the uncertainty-based logic developed in this chapter, eminently exploitable. We have nothing to fear from them, now or in the future. If we are to be persuaded to treat them fairly nonetheless, the appeal must be to some different sort of logic altogether.[44] It is that alternative logic which forms the subject of the next chapter.

41 They will not literally turn black, to be sure. But ethnic politics might turn sour, in ways that might have much the same effects for Polish-Americans, etc., for example.
42 Rose 1976a. The difference is that Southern blacks had Northern allies. More will be said on that subject in the next chapter .
43 Lijphart 1977, pp. 147–50.
44 We might still talk, then, of a "veil of ignorance." But since there we must assume instead that people are motivated by the desire to act morally already – to "reach agreement on reasonable terms" and such like – "a veil of ignorance is an optional feature," nothing more than "a heuristic device which can be resorted to on occasion" for dramatic effect, but which "does not have to be relied on to create solutions" in the derivations (Barry 1989, p. 331).

FOUR

Non-exploitation

The previous two chapters have been devoted to exploring ways in which people might be motivated to act relatively directly upon Golden Rule precepts. They might be led to do so either by simple reciprocity or by uncertainty, which serves as its over-time analog. In the first case, you do unto others as you would have them do unto you because you are pretty sure that the tables will indeed be turned. In the second case, you do so because you have good reason to fear that they may well be turned, and that is enough.

Appealing relatively directly to the Golden Rule in such ways is an attractive strategy. It establishes a fairly tight link between moral belief and moral motivation: we are led to perform morally proper acts out of considerations very closely akin to those that made us think that those were the morally proper acts to perform in the first place. The link thus forged between moral belief and moral action is, in this way, relatively direct; and the appeal to people's "sense of morality" as a motivating force is kept down to a bare minimum.

That is a good trick where we can pull it off, and often we can. Sometimes, though, we cannot. There are some people who are not now, and most probably never will be, in a position to help or to harm us. And so long as we can be really pretty certain of that fact, neither reciprocity nor even uncertainty will give us any compelling reason for taking their interests seriously into account when framing our own actions. Reciprocity or uncertainty might force an attitude of impartial concern upon us with regard to those people who might someday be in a position to retaliate. Those who never will be in such a position, however, lie beyond the pale of reciprocity or uncertainty-based rationales for impartiality.

This point has been brought home to contemporary philosophers most powerfully in connection with John Rawls's reinvocation of David Hume's analysis of "the circumstances of justice."[1] Hume's idea is that notions of distributive justice only make sense in certain sorts of circumstances. One such circumstance is "moderate Scarcity": there would be no need for rules to govern the distribution of things that are so abundant that everyone could have all that he could possibly want of them anyway; and, conversely, in circumstances of really dire scarcity there would be no future for rules governing distributions either, since people would inevitably ignore the rules rather than starve. Another of the Humean circumstances of justice is "moderate benevolence": if people were so altruistic as always to put others' interests first, or even always to put others' interests fully on a par with their own, then they would have fully internalized norms of justice already and would not need to have social norms externally imposed upon them; if, conversely, people were so selfish as to refuse ever to take any regard whatsoever of the interests of others, then once again norms of justice could get no grip on them.

Now, for Hume as for Rawls, the "circumstances" referred to in the phrase "circumstances of justice" are meant to be objective circumstances located in the external world. Norms of morality – norms of justice and such like – can arise only where the world really is arranged in such a way as to make goods moderately scarce and to make people moderately benevolent.

What these external circumstances are that make people "moderately benevolent" is, for Hume at least, clearly just circumstances giving rise to a real threat of retaliation on the part of those whom you might have mistreated. Hume invites us to engage in this mental experiment. Let us ask ourselves

---

1   Hume 1777, sect. 3, pt 1; see also 1739, bk 3, pt 2, sect. 2; 1777, sect. 3, pt 1. This is the way these themes have been picked up by Rawls 1971, sect 22 and by Hart 1961, pp. 189–95 before him, anyway. For critiques, see Barry 1978, pp. 220–23; 1989, chaps 4 and 5 and Goodin 1982, pp. 77–8.

what would happen to our notions of justice and morality, "were there a species of creatures intermingled with men, which, though rational, were possessed of such inferior strength, both of body and mind, that they were incapable of all resistance, and could never, upon the highest provocation, make us feel the effects of their resentment; the necessary consequence," as Hume conceives it, "is that we should . . . not, properly speaking, lie under any restraint of justice with regard to them. . . . Our intercourse with them could not be called society, which supposes a degree of equality; but absolute command on one side, and servile obedience on the other. Whatever we covet, they must instantly resign . . . ." And since "no inconvenience ever results from the exercise of a power, so firmly established in nature," Hume concludes that "the restraints of justice and property" would be "totally useless" and "never have [a] place in so unequal a confederacy."[2]

Although constraints of justice – understood as direct or even extended reciprocity – fail us in these circumstances, Hume nonetheless thinks that we are under certain moral obligations with respect to these people. He would not describe these obligations in terms of "justice," strictly speaking. But he is at pains to say that "we should be bound by the laws of humanity to give gentle usage to those creatures." We should treat them with "compassion and kindness"; we should be bound by "restraints of humanity" in our dealings with them.[3] There is no way in which such utterly helpless creatures as this could force us to do so. But, morally, we ought do so nonetheless.

The norm to which such sentiments appeal is that the strong, in general, have a particular duty to protect the weak. More precisely, the principle at work here is one that holds that those who are in a position of power *vis-à-vis* others are, by virtue of that position of power, under a special obligation to protect and not to exploit the others who are particularly vulnerable to and dependent upon them.[4]

2 Hume 1777, sect. 3, pt 1, p. 152.
3 Ibid.
4 Goodin 1985a, b. Strictly speaking, this is a two-part duty involving: "firstly . . . a general duty to suspend ordinary rules of behavior in

That is standardly phrased as a principle of "non-exploitation," which is standardly spelled out in turn as requiring that we refrain from taking "unfair advantage" of others.[5] That explication is less helpful than it might be, of course: it just pushes all the hard problems back into questions of what sorts of advantage-taking count as "unfair." But even with those questions left hanging, the phrase is still at least partially illuminating. It focuses our attention starkly on the fact that problems of exploitation arise, somehow or another, from having an advantage and pressing it.

At least in certain circumstances, at least with regard to certain sorts of advantages, then, it is wrong – exploitative – to press an advantage you might have over others. That in itself is a useful discovery, even ahead of explicating the precise circumstances in which pressing your advantage would be wrong. It means, at the very least, that bargaining behavior – market morality and its political analog – cannot be a universally permissible practice.

Market morality tells you always to strike as hard a bargain as you can, and to press any advantage that falls your way to the hilt. The logic of seeing politics, analogously, as a competitive market for votes would similarly require that you squeeze out all superfluous members from your coalition.[6] The principle of non-exploitation, even without further explication, tells us that there are certain circumstances, at least, in which it would be wrong for you to do so. At least in circumstances of great power disparities, the strong are obliged to protect and not to exploit the weak.

It is easy enough to see how some norm – partial though it may be as a moral code – would fall out of general Golden Rule style thinking. Presumably those who are presently in positions of power would want others to protect rather than exploit them, likewise, were the tables turned.[7] The trick lies

---

dealing with" them, most especially by not "pressing your advantage against them in the way that would have been perfectly permissible in ordinary everyday relationships"; and, "secondly . . . a duty to take positive measures to assist" such people (Goodin 1988b, p. 149).

5 Goodin 1988b, chap. 5.
6 Goodin 1988a. Riker 1962. Shapley 1967.
7 Of course, both may well wish, above all else, not to have to depend upon others for protection. That is what I meant by saying that the

less in morally justifying this principle than in making it motivationally compelling.

The necessary motivation might, of course, be provided by the sorts of considerations already discussed. Notions of reciprocity, of a sort, clearly have a role here. Norms of non-exploitation sometimes simply mark the limits of how far the strong can safely press their advantages against the weak without provoking undue resistance from them; and everything from eighteenth-century English bread riots to twentieth-century Southeast Asian peasant rebellions has been traced to violation of those norms.[8] Insofar as the strong have something of that sort to fear from the weak, the motivation on the part of the strong to comply with those norms can be wholly explained in terms of retaliation and reciprocity, already discussed.

Alternatively, a variation on the uncertainty theme already discussed might be at work behind compliance with non-exploitation norms. Even if you know you need nothing from particular others just now, you never know when you might. Thus, Gunnar Myrdal takes pleasure in quoting a 1942 *New York Times* editorial to the effect that American blacks may have been safely exploitable before the war, but that that exploitation was now compromising American efforts to recruit allies among non-white peoples abroad:

> The Chinese, the East Indians, the numerous African peoples and many other groups are on our side, or would

---

principle is a very partial one: it does not say that it is right for there to be some who are strong and others who are weak; it merely says that, if there are strong and weak, it is right for the strong to protect the weak.

8　Thompson 1971. Scott 1976. Hobsbawm (1985, p. 26) analyses the activities of "social bandits" across a wide range of times and places similarly: "They right wrongs, they correct and avenge cases of injustice, and in so doing apply a more general criterion of just and fair relations between men in general, and especially between the rich and the poor, the strong and the weak. This is a modest aim, which leaves the rich to exploit the poor (but no more than is traditionally accepted as 'fair'), the strong to oppress the weak (but within the limits of what is equitable, and mindful of their social and moral duties). It demands not that there should be no more lords, or even the lords should not be expected to take their serfs' women, but only that when they did, they should not shirk the obligation to give their bastards an education."

be so if they were completely convinced that we mean what we say by equality. . . . But we Americans cannot very well talk convincingly in these terms unless we prove our sincerity in our own country.[9]

Myrdal's point, of course, is how that consideration led to better treatment of the American black during and after the war. But perhaps the anticipation of that sort of problem – the uncertainty over whether we really can exploit the black all that safely – might have made white America rather more cautious in exploiting the black before the war as well.[10]

It would be wrong to underestimate the extent to which those more familiar considerations of reciprocity or uncertainty might help secure compliance with norms of non-exploitation. These may well be the most standard ways in which compliance is obtained. But those forces have already been discussed. For purposes of the present discussion, let us therefore bracket them out, to see if there is any other way of securing non-exploitation left when neither of those other two mechanisms can work to guarantee it.

Suppose for the sake of this argument, then, that the strong can be really pretty confident that no retaliation will be forthcoming if they were to exploit members of a certain group. Morally, they might agree that they should not exploit them, nonetheless. The strong may well agree that they would not want others to exploit them, were the tables turned; but in the circumstances here envisaged, they can pretty well count on the tables not being turned. How, then, can we get the strong to put themselves imaginatively into the shoes of the weak, when they know fully well that they will never actually be there?

9 Editorial, *New York Times*, 3 April 1942, quoted in Myrdal 1944, p. 1068.
10 In the first instance, it was the support of non-white allies abroad that the US needed, and blacks in America itself got better treatment merely as a side-effect of that. But the same "law of anticipated reactions" ended up giving black Americans themselves more bargaining leverage in dealings with white America, once it became clear to all concerned that the US could not count on needed support for the war effort abroad without treating blacks better at home.

In attempting to answer that question, let us consider some actual cases of gross power disparities, to see what sorts of norms actually governed interactions there and how those norms actually got a motivational hold on people in them. In so doing, of course, we run the risk of romanticizing what were, in truth, some truly hideous circumstances. That is not the intention. Clearly, slavery would have been a perfectly awful institution, even if all slaveowners kept to the code of not (overly) exploiting their slaves; and, equally clearly, not all slaveowners kept to even that minimal code.

Still, there is surely something to be learned from the examination of cases of only partial compliance with only minimally demanding moral codes. That may not seem like much. But remember the circumstances here in view: those who had and could be pretty confident of retaining power did not have to do even that much. Seeing what has made people act even minimally morally, when they did not have to do so, might help us see how to make people act yet more morally in the future, under similarly unpromising circumstances.

With that partial apology in place, let us turn to the cases themselves. The first example concerns the case of slavery in the American South. Formally, slaveowners were legally at liberty to do just about anything they liked to their slaves, right up to the eve of the Civil War. Certainly they had legal power to "discipline" them as they saw fit; and even when laws against murdering or maiming slaves were finally introduced in the latter part of the period, those laws were rendered largely dead letters by the need to find whites who were in a position to be able to testify to the offense.[11] In effect, then, slaveowners were absolute masters of their slaves. Formally, they were by and large able to do with their slaves whatever they willed.

Informally, though, slaveowners were honor-bound to a fairly strict code of more decent conduct toward their charges. Some describe the code in terms of paternalism, others in terms of chivalry.[12] But in truth it was little more than what has here been described as the principle of non-exploitation, the duty laid upon the particularly powerful to protect and not exploit the particularly weak. That is all that the Charleston,

11   Stampp 1964, pp. 142, 183, 189, 212–18. Genovese 1974, pp. 37, 40–9.
12   Genovese 1974, pp. 3–7. Patterson 1982, p. 94.

South Carolina, theology professor seems to have had in mind when saying, on the eve of the Civil War, that the relationship was a "moral" one. The code of reciprocal rights and duties, as he described it, was based on the proposition that "our slaves are our solemn trust. . . . While we have a right to use and direct their labors, we are bound to feed, clothe and protect them."[13]

Now, there may well be a temptation to dismiss those as the sanctimonious pieties of theology professors. The point, however, remains that precisely those obligations were standardly included by slaveowners themselves in written instructions given to their overseers for the day-to-day management of their slaves; and eventually they found their way into the legal codes of the various slave states themselves.[14] However well or poorly they might have been enforced, that those injunctions were promulgated at all is an important symbolic act that is powerfully indicative of community self-perceptions.

Those community standards, in turn, were brought powerfully to bear upon slaveowners themselves through the code of "honour" that seems to characterize all slave-owning societies.[15] Kenneth Stampp describes the slaveowner's side of the *Peculiar Institution* as follows:

> A master who gave some thought to his standing in the community certainly wished to avoid a reputation for inordinate cruelty. To be counted a true Southern Gentleman he had to be humane to his bondsmen, to exercise self-control in dealing with them, to know how to give commands without raising his voice.[16]

Two things about that code seem remarkable. One is the extent to which the rest of the community was inclined to censure (at least by remarking unkindly upon) violations of that standard.[17] The other is the way in which so many slaveholders actually "met the test with remarkable success."[18]

Let us not exaggerate. Certainly it was not true that all

13 The Reverend Dr Thornwell, quoted in Genovese 1974, p. 76.
14 Ibid., pp. 37–49, 75–86.
15 Patterson 1982, chap. 3. Wyatt-Brown 1982, esp. chap. 14.
16 Stampp 1964, p. 176.
17 Ibid. pp. 176–7, 212–18. Genovese 1974, pp. 37–49, 75–86.
18 Stampp 1964, p. 176.

slaveowners were "good massas," nor was it true that life even under a "good massa" was without cruelty practiced at regular intervals. Neither is it the case that high moral notions of honor and chivalry were all that kept masters from beating their slaves: after all, they were valuable capital investments.[19]

Still, with all those caveats firmly in place, the larger point nonetheless remains that even among communities of slaveowners there is some minimal appreciation of the moral force of the Golden Rule. Even within the broader context of gross exploitation of one person by another, slaveowners can come to some minimal appreciation of the way in which power implies duties. And even slaveowners are prepared to enforce those minimal – very minimal – duties of non-exploitation upon one another. There was no external reason to do so, particularly. There was no threat that slaveowners would, any time during their lives, become slaves themselves. (Even the most seriously aggrieved could hardly describe Reconstruction in those terms.) But even without the threat of reciprocal treatment, they still saw the point of the principle. Without wishing to praise slaveowners, particularly, it ought to be said that it is a real testament to the depth of the sense of morality that is rooted in human nature that even slaveowners can be made to feel its force.

A second example concerns the way in which European settlers treated the original Indian inhabitants of the North American continent – the clearest example that Hume himself could offer of one people being utterly at the mercy of another, and completely beyond the bounds of justice-as-reciprocity for that reason.[20] Again, let us not understate the shame and horror of that history. Leave aside all the unauthorized atrocities committed by bands of frontiersmen acting on their own; leave aside the natural excesses inevitably committed in the course of the many Indian wars. Official government policy in ostensibly settled times was evil enough. As part of the official policy of Indian removal, "one hundred thousand Indians were removed from their homes and transported west of the Mississippi" River between 1820 and 1844; "one-quarter died or were killed on the way."[21]

19 Ibid., pp. 162, 177. Genovese 1974, p. 43.
20 Hume 1777, sect. 3, pt 1, p. 152.
21 Rogin 1971, pp. 270–1. See further Barsh and Henderson 1980.

It is an outrageous history, to be sure. But, in a way, it is an utterly unsurprising one. What else would you expect, Hume might ask, when one group has something that another wants and is powerless to prevent it from taking? That does not justify the theft of lands, in any sense. Still less does it justify or even, come to that, explain the gratuitous cruelties practiced as part of it.

In our revulsion at the larger picture, though, we should not be blinded to some curious things going on down in one small corner of the frame. The settlers, at least occasionally, seemed to have pangs of conscience about what they were doing. It was not only in talking to the tribes that they evoked the image of the Great White Father; in talking amongst themselves, too, it was hard to shake off altogether the sense of paternalistic duties owed by strong fathers to weak dependents. Thus, President John Qunicy Adams's Secretary of State is found declaring,

> In their present destitute and deplorable condition, . . . which is constantly growing more hopeless, it would seem to be not only the right but the duty of the government to take them under its paternal care, and to exercise over their persons and property the salutory rights and duties of guardianship.[22]

And even Martin Van Buren – Andrew Jackson's Vice President and designated successor – is found saying:

> We are as a nation responsible [for] . . . the course we have pursued and shall pursue towards a people comparatively weak, upon whom we were perhaps in the beginning unjustifiable aggressors, but of whom, in the progress of time and events, we have become the guardians, and, as we hope, the benefactors.[23]

Again, what is striking is not so much that these pieties were mouthed but rather that they were adopted and enforced,

22 P. B. Porter, quoted in Rogin 1971, p. 290; there, in a footnote, Rogin pointedly adds, "It would be greatly in error to think that the language of fathers and children was used only in communicating to the Indians, not when whites addressed the problem among themselves."
23 Quoted in ibid., p. 272.

however imperfectly, as community standards. Perhaps the most crucial factor here is the way in which this view of the Indian tribes as "domestic dependent nations" or "dependent wards" came to dominate US Supreme Court decisions. Chief Justice John Marshall's opinion in the 1831 case of the *Cherokee Nation v. Georgia* set the pattern, saying the Indians "are in a state of pupilage; their relation to the United States resembles that of a ward to his guardian."[24] And that way of talking dominated court opinions right down to the New Deal era. Time and again, we find the power and the duty of the federal government to protect Indians being traced by the Court to the Indians" relationship of dependency upon white Americans. An 1885 opinion, typical of the kind, held that:

> These Indian tribes *are* wards of the Nation. They are communities *dependent* on the United States; dependent largely for their daily food; dependent for their political rights. . . . From their very weakness and helplessness . . . there arises the duty of protection, and with it the power. This has always been recognized by the Executive and by Congress, and by this Court whenever the question has arisen.[25]

Now, again, we must not overestimate the power of courts in Washington to dictate events at frontier outposts. Most of these cases, note, grew out of attempts by the federal government to stop state governments from abusing the Indians resident in the state. Equally notably, these actions were not brought by Indians themselves petitioning for the food and blankets that were legally and morally due them under such doctrines but were instead brought by the federal government, seeking to assert its claim of authority over both state governments and Indian nations.[26] So we must not be lulled into the

24 Marshall 1831, p. 17.
25 Miller 1885, p. 384; see similarly Mathews 1886, p. 28. See more generally Barsh and Henderson 1980, chap. 8 and Goodin 1985a, p. 40.
26 Indeed, if the fiduciary model ostensibly underlying these arguments were taken seriously, the sovereign prerogatives of Indian nations would be much more fully protected than actually they are under decisions that purport to appeal, through notions of "dependency," to those models. See Anon. 1987.

illusion that American Indians were treated decently, at least after they had been decisively beaten into submission.

Still, once again, it seems impressive testimony to the sense of morality rooted in human nature that even butchers should come to some minimal appreciation of the force of the Golden Rule in this way. They no longer had anything much to fear from the subjugated people. But at precisely that point, they came to internalize – however imperfectly – principles of non-exploitation and the duties that the strong owe to the weak. Indeed, they internalized those principles not only with the force of law (for, as cynics would say, what was law worth on the frontier?) but with the force of higher law. Even the Supreme Court, as adjudicator of America's most sacred values, talked in those tones. Talk may be cheap, but talking in those elevated tones is never altogether free of further commitments to practical action.[27]

The other example that sprang most immediately to Hume's mind of a people who were utterly at the mercy of others – and to whom principles of justice-as-reciprocity would not naturally apply – were wives.[28] Right through Victorian times, the vast majority of women were to be utterly dependent upon their menfolk (fathers, husbands, or brothers) for even their barest necessities.

Why that was so need not detain us here. Women's dependency was traditionally rationalized in terms of their nature: their "permanent inferiority of strength, and occasional loss of [working] time in gestation and rearing of infants" and such like.[29] The truth of the matter, of course, is that those "facts" are not natural facts but rather social facts about the law and the labor market. Marriage and property law made a wife dependent upon her husband, by subsuming her legal personality within his; and the only jobs effectively open to women on the open labor market were "the very lowest," providing insufficient means for independent support.[30] But all that is, from the present perspective, purely a side issue.

Why women were dependent does not matter so much, for

---

27 Goodin 1980, chap. 5.
28 Hume 1777, sect. 3, pt 1, p. 152.
29 Cf. Thompson 1825, p. x and Mill 1869, chap. 2.
30 Thompson 1825, pp. xi, 57. Mill 1869, chap. 2. See further Goodin 1985a, pp. 70–9 and Pateman 1988, chaps 5 and 6.

purposes of my present story, as what followed from the fact of their dependency in terms of moral sociology. There arose a very strong norm – admittedly honored all too often in the breach – that those of the weaker sex deserved especially gentle and solicitous treatment, purely on account of their presumed weakness. Of course, that is not to say that wife-beating never happened, for example, or that it was always punished when it did. But the point remains that it was a particularly shameful thing to have done.[31]

That was not merely a norm of private ethics either. Much public policy (for better or worse) was predicated upon precisely such norms. The famous Brandeis brief, so crucial in persuading the US Supreme Court to approve laws restricting the exploitative hours that women laborers had been forced to work at the turn of the century, argued precisely in these terms. The emphasis was decidedly on the peculiar weakness of women's constitutions and on their utter dependence upon men for their protection.[32]

No doubt those attitudes – always unwarranted, in any objective sense – have proven singularly unhelpful in contemporary struggles to secure a stronger foothold for women in the contemporary labor market. The only reason for raising such sensitive (and possibly even offensive) subjects at all is simply to point out this curious anomaly. At precisely the same time that men thought that they had women utterly at their mercy, they simultaneously renounced the pursuit of that advantage. Officially, at least, they internalized what would seem to be strong norms against pressing their presumed advantage against the "weaker sex."

Whether or not they were right in thinking that they enjoyed such absolute power over women is another matter. The

31 In his letters to newspapers, Mill continually complained that domestic violence tended to be laughed off rather lightly, as Alan Ryan rightly reminds me; and no doubt it is true that he thought that Victorians should take an even dimmer view of the practice than some of them did. But there is powerful internal evidence in his *Subjection of Women* that Mill (1869, chap. 2) supposed Victorian morals to be powerfully opposed to the practice. One of the most rhetorically powerful devices he employs in arguing for reform of the marriage contract in general, and for legalizing divorce in particular, is that only by thus equalizing power relations within the marriage can women defend themselves against domestic violence.

32 Brewer 1908, pp. 421–2.

interesting thing, for present purposes, is that even – indeed, especially – when they thought that they did, they were firmly persuaded that as a purely moral and not at all prudential matter they simply should not use it. That even the most chauvinist can feel the force of Golden Rule morality even to this minimal extent – conceding that he ought not exploit women, even while he is in the process of oppressing them – is again dramatic testimony to the hold that this norm of non-exploitation seems to have in human nature.

L et us now try to stand back from those particular examples and see what lessons might be learned from them. The first thing that must be said – yet again – is that it is obviously better to prevent exploitable situations from arising than it is to block exploitation in such situations once they have arisen. Non-exploitation is, at best, only a very partial application of Golden Rule logic.

It bears repeating, loudly and often, that the great inequalities of power which are here seen as giving rise to the need for norms of non-exploitation are virtually all artificial rather than natural in their origins. It bears repeating, loudly and often, that a much better response in virtually all those cases would be to strive to eliminate not so much exploitation itself as the conditions that made exploitation a real risk in the first place. Insofar as those inequalities of power making exploitation possible were socially created and sustained, perhaps they could be socially eliminated as well.[33]

That goal – the elimination of involuntary dependencies – ought to be our highest moral goal, in this regard. Norms of non-exploitation ought clearly to be seen as second-best rules, for application to situations in which that ideal is, for one reason or another, unattainable. To say that a norm of non-exploitation is second-best is not to say that it is morally unimportant, though. Quite the contrary, where it is needed it is *really* needed. In the non-ideal world of great inequalities of power, it is more important – not less – that people be somehow bound by the canons of Golden Rule morality, even imperfectly applied.

The preceding examples have shown that, historically, we have internalized (with varying degrees of success) norms

33 Goodin 1985a, chap. 7.

against exploiting various people who were very much at the mercy of our own arbitrary wills: slaves, Indians, wives. That we did so is an undeniably mixed blessing. But although the blessing was undeniably mixed, it was undeniably a blessing as well.

The use to which those examples will here be put parallels Thomas Nagel's proof of *The Possibility of Altruism*.[34] Schematically, Nagel's argument is this. Usually we think that saving for our own future is not at all an act of altruism. It is instead a prudent act of the most purely self-interested sort. But on one very plausible view of personal identity – the view that traces personal identity to "mental connectedness" – your "future self" actually does differ, perhaps substantially, from your present self. And if that is so, then saving for your own future consumption would actually count as an altruistic transfer from one person (your present self) to another (your rather different future self). We nonetheless regularly find it within ourselves to practice that particular form of intra-personal altruism. And the fact that we do might be taken as evidence that we have it within ourselves to act atruistically toward others more generally. Or so Nagel's argument goes.

The argument to be developed here is analogous to that one. Where Nagel builds on the observation that people's motivational structure permits them to save for their own future, my argument here builds on the fact that people's motivational structure is consistent with their respecting norms against exploitation of slaves, Indians, and wives.[35] Historically, we seem to have been able to find it within ourselves to internalize norms of fair dealing with those who are utterly at our mercy, and who cannot help or harm us in any important way.[36] And

34 Nagel 1970, building on a suggestion in Sidgwick 1907, bk 4, chap. 2, p. 418.
35 To those examples might be added the still more dramatic one of the rescuers of Jews in Nazi Europe. They, too, were responding – at least in part – to the helplessness of those particular Jews dependent upon them for protection from the Nazis (Monore, Barton, and Klingemann 1991). And they were doing so in circumstances in which the risks and potential costs of protecting the vulnerable amounted to far more than the costs of forgoing opportunities for pressing bargaining advantages against weak opponents.
36 In some circumstances, prevailing norms do seem to permit one side to press its advantages to the hilt. Conspicuously among them are cases

that we have done so shows that there is, motivationally, something within us that would enable us to practice a rule of non-exploitation more generally. There is, apparently, within us a sense of morality that will usually stretch to a norm of non-exploitation, at least in cases of dramatic disparities in power.

Most of the work that remains to be done, that having been said, is essentially bridging work. The task is to work from particularly striking cases like those of slaves, Indians, and Victorian wives to other, less striking examples in which the dependency, although no less severe, is less obvious because it is somehow more impersonal. The Third World famine victim is no less dependent upon the First World for help than is the Victorian wife on her husband: and wage-earners collectively are no less dependent upon employers collectively for sustenance than are slaves on their masters.[37] But those are relatively impersonal dependency relationships, in contrast to the more one-to-one dependencies to which our notions of non-exploitation more naturally seem to apply. And it is harder to see that the same rules should apply and how exactly they should apply in those other sorts of settings.

There are, in fact, two ways of carrying out this bridging operation. One of them works, in effect, by bridging up from particular cases to a general principle, and then back down again. Let us call that the "ratcheting up" strategy. Suppose you feel the force of the argument that you should protect and not exploit particular sorts of people (like slaves, vanquished tribes, Victorian wives, etc.).[38] Suppose, casting around for some general principle capable of subsuming all those

---

involving bargaining in the shadow of adjudication – between parties to a civil suit, prosecutors and accused, insurance companies and clients, and so on (Genn 1987, pp. 132–3, 163–9; Fiss 1984). But in all such cases, what seems crucial is the "adversary system" excuse: the fact that all parties alike are represented by legal counsel creates the illusion that neither really is utterly at the mercy of the other, at all (cf. Luban 1988, pt 1).

37 "Collectively," because of course any given individual might go to work for another employer. But the one group, as a whole, is utterly dependent upon the other, as a whole.

38 Or, for another example, starving peasants in times of drought: on the Indian system of grain distribution through "fair price shops" in times of crop failure, see Torry 1986, pp. 15–17.

apparently analogous cases, you discover that the salient fact in your thinking about each of those cases is that we are just so much stronger than those other people. That, you discover, is what makes you think that it would be wrong for us to press our advantage against them in ordinary bargaining. Then reflection upon particular cases will have led you to endorse a general rule – phrased negatively as a rule of "non-exploitation," positively as one of "protecting the vulnerable" – that can then be applied to various other cases which are formally analogous to those, but about which you have no immediate moral intuitions (or perhaps even contrary initial predispositions). Provided you are prepared to see your moral responses to particular cases as part of a general pattern at all, you can in this way be brought around to extending the scope of your moral concerns.[39]

How well the strategy will work depends, obviously, upon how compelling people find the analogy. Here, too, there is a large body of social psychological literature upon which we might build.[40] Perhaps the lessons of rhetoric might be more useful than those of psychology here, though. Whether or not people recognize an analogy as apt depends, much more than on logic or psychology, upon the "narrative art of story-telling." Only if they can see themselves in the story, and see the relevance of the parable to other analogous situations in which they actually find themselves, will people find themselves moved by the tale. And whether you can be made to "see yourself in the story," in that way, depends very largely upon the rhetorical success of the story.[41]

The second way of carrying out this bridging operation works by bridging down from general principles. In this case, people already endorse certain ethical principles of a very broad or abstract sort. The problem lies just in seeing what those principles might mean for particular cases. People are committed, intuitively, to certain very general standards of "fairness," for example. But they are very uncertain how, exactly, those standards might apply to problems of pricing or regulation of public utilities or whatever.[42] The task here lies

39   That is the strategy I pursue in Goodin 1985a, b.
40   See Tversky 1977 and the further sources cited therein.
41   Lakoff and Johnson 1980. I am grateful to Willem Witteveen for enlightening discussions around these themes.
42   Zajac 1985.

less in motivating people to abide by the dictates of the general principle of "fairness," whatever they might be; it is more a matter of helping them to see what its dictates are. Even in this relatively more modest task of merely explicating the requirements of a general principle, reflection upon analogous cases might be helpful, however. The point of calling the wage laborer a "wage slave," for example, is to help people who are clear about the implications of their general moral principles for the case of slavery to see what the same principles would imply for the capitalist employment relationship.[43]

The story about what is wrong with exploitation can be told either way, or both ways at once. What ought to be pointed out in the present context is just this: either telling of the tale depends, for any motivational hold it gets on people, upon a sense of morality that people have already internalized; they must already be able to see that at least certain sorts of exploitation (of slaves, vanquished Indian tribes, Victorian wives, or whomever) is wrong. We can motivate people to act morally – at least minimally morally, in the sense of non-exploitatively – by building upon such sentiments. But all available strategies for doing so really do presuppose that those sorts of sentiments are already present, somehow or another, in their motivate structure.

It is an error – a common error, to be sure, but an error nonetheless – to suppose that our sole concern with exploitation is with economic exploitation. Lovers and friends, colleagues and neighbors can exploit one another, just as surely as can economic classes. And this more personal side of exploitation occasionally spills over into public policy, as for example when we decide to ban pornography or prostitution on the grounds that it tends to exploit (as well as degrade) those engaged in it.[44]

Still it must surely be true that our primary concern with exploitation inevitably is with its economic form. In closing, therefore, let us reflect briefly upon some recent psychological

43 Similarly, when Ransom and Sutch (1977, chap. 8) refer to the relations between freed slaves and local merchants upon whom they relied for credit as one of "debt peonage," they are emphasizing that the same reasons for giving the slaves "one kind of freedom" should make us want to give them other kinds as well.
44 Goodin 1988b, chap. 5. Pateman 1988, chap. 7.

experiments revealing that people have some surprisingly nuanced views about when it is and is not proper for people to press ordinary market advantages that they might have.

Perhaps it is a bit grand to call these findings of "experiments" at all. Actually, they are just responses to questions, put to some hundred or so people during telephone interviews. The interviewer first described some economic situation in relatively homely commercial terms – the shortage of Cabbage Patch dolls in the shops one Christmas, for example. Respondents were then asked whether they thought certain sort of behavior in that situation (typically, increasing the price) was fair or not.

What comes across pretty clearly in those interviews, for what they are worth, is that people seem systematically to disapprove of what they perceive as exploitation of unusually strong market positions. They regard it as unfair for an employer to exploit an excess in the supply of labor to cut wages. They regard it as unfair for shops to exploit a temporary shortage of commodities by raising prices, even when close substitutes for those commodities are readily available. They regard it as unfair for a landlord to increase the rent of a tenant who has recently taken a job nearby and is therefore unlikely to move in consequence. They regard it as unfair for a personnel officer to ask the four qualified candidates for a job in an area of high unemployment to state the lowest salary that they could accept, and then to hire the one asking for the lowest salary.[45] In short, it is widely (typically, by margins of 2 or 3 to 1) perceived to be unacceptable for economic agents to exploit unusual market power for commercial advantage.

Now, that may be a long way, still, from constituting widespread popular assent to the central elements of the Marxian indictment of the capitalist mode of production. Or it

45 Kahneman, Knetsch, and Thaler 1986b, pp. 730, 734–6; see similarly Kahneman, Knetsch, and Thaler 1986a for another report of the same experiments. Lest popular opinion in these matters be thought – as it might, by economists – to reflect completely unreflective prejudice, consider the similar judgments offered in Sidgwick's *Principles of Political Economy*. There, he writes that it is wrong to charge over the competitive price for a commodity, just because there is an especially urgent need for the commodity and there is no competition in supplying it (Sidgwick 1883, bk 3, chap. 9, pp. 585–6). That was at least arguably all that canon law principles of "just price" ever meant, too (Berman 1983, pp. 247–8).

may not. It all depends upon what you see as lying at the center of that analysis. And those who place the "reserve army of the unemployed" at the center of the picture might be rather more inclined to take heart from these findings than would some others.[46]

The point of introducing these findings is just to show that people do, by and large, have some "sense of morality" in these matters with which we can work. Just as we might be able to ratchet up from their intuitive sense of the wrongfulness of exploiting slaves to more general principles of social exploitation, so too might we be able to ratchet up from their intuitive sense of the wrongfulness of price-gouging in the trade for Cabbage Patch dolls to more general principles of economic exploitation.

To say that it is possible, though, is not necessarily to say that it is going to be easy. A lot of ratcheting might be required. Still, at least there seems to be some hope of motivating people in this way to do something about broader patterns of economic exploitation, just as we have already managed to motivate them to do something about narrower forms of social exploitation.

46 See, e.g., Elster 1978.

PART II
The Political Tack

FIVE

Extending the Franchise

In the moral realm, reciprocity seems the most direct instantiation of Golden Rule morality. There, what motivates you to "do unto others as you would have them do unto you" is the simple thought that "they will." The two propositions do not capture precisely the same thought, to be sure. But the thought which leads one to perform the morally-worthy act is at least first cousin to the thought which leads one to think that it is morally the right act to perform, on Golden Rule grounds, in the first place.

"One person, one vote" is the analogue within the political realm of that model of reciprocity in the moral realm. The equality of voting rights, conjoined as it typically is with broadly democratic procedures for aggregating votes and the competition for votes that follows from such procedures, goes a long way towards ensuring that others actually will (sooner or later) be in a position to do unto you as you have done unto them.[1]

That thought is probably what is responsible for tempering democratic politics and leading it down more morally acceptable, Golden Rule paths. In this case, once again, broadly the same thought leads us both to pursue the morally more

---

1 Strictly speaking, putting the point in terms of "ensuring" that outcome is unnecessarily strong. Engendering substantial uncertainty on the subject is often enough. More will be said on this score in chapter 6 below.

desirable course of action (here, the politically more moderate course) and also to think that, morally, that is the right course of action.

Reciprocity proves a compelling reason to do unto others, however, only if they may someday be in a position to do unto you in turn. Those within our own society (or outside it) who have no power to help or to harm us would, on this model, be in no position to command decent treatment from us. Neither in the more narrowly political terms of the present chapter would those who find themselves electorally disen-franchised. The threat of reciprocal retaliation at the next election might give one set of electors good reason for treating other *electors* fairly. But no one has anything to fear – in purely electoral terms, at least – from those who stand outside the electorate.

The thought underlying reciprocity as a model of how to motivate compliance with Golden Rule morality in general is that the tables might turn, socially. You might tomorrow come to need assistance from those who need your assistance today. The parallel thought underlying the political analog is that the tables might turn, politically. Today's winners might become tomorrow's losers, and you might tomorrow find yourself politically at the mercy of those who are politically at your mercy today.[2]

Tables can turn only among those who are actual players in the game, though. If someone is not in the game at all, then there is no prospect of his coming out on top of it in the next round. So, on the face of it, this looks like a potentially compelling argument for abiding by the Golden Rule ethic with respect to everyone who already has the vote. But it looks like no kind of argument at all for extending the franchise to those not presently entitled to vote.

The fact of the matter is, of course, that the electoral franchise has been extended steadily over time and with increasing rapidity over the last century and a half. No doubt such electoral reforms are morally laudatory. They give politi-cal power to otherwise powerless people, and those people are typically among the most socially and economically disadvan-

2   This thought has been formalized mathematically by Rae (1969) and Taylor (1969), in ways discussed in chapter 6 below.

taged as well. Using the political leverage that comes with the vote, those disadvantaged members of society can press far more effectively for improvements in their quality of life, across the board.

That is just to say that extending the franchise furthers the ends of Golden Rule morality – and it does so, furthermore, in ways wholly explicable in the minimally moralized terms of simple reciprocity. Once people have the vote, little direct appeal to people's moral principles is required in getting others to take their interests seriously, even if not quite to consider them completely on a par with their own. Still, the thought that today's winners might be tomorrow's losers should suffice to dissuade people from voting burdens onto others that they would not be prepared to bear themselves.[3] And it should do so for the most self-interested of reasons: the burdens you vote onto others today they will quite possibly vote onto you tomorrow.

But if it is true that direct appeals to people's moral principles are minimally required once the franchise has been extended, it is equally true that such extensions of the franchise themselves must surely require a hefty dose of precisely such direct moral appeals to people's moral principles. At least the particular strategy presently under discussion – relying as it does upon threats of reciprocal retaliation – certainly will not, it seems, suffice to motivate the sharing of political power with those who are presently politically powerless.

In this chapter, I propose to examine the history of campaigns to extend the franchise and arguments used in the course of them to see to what extent this natural supposition has actually proven true. Some of the arguments amounted to purely moral appeals, to be sure. But some of them amount to an appeal to the logic of reciprocity, albeit at one remove. So even in extending the franchise – as well as in the everyday exercising of it – the minimally moralized model of threats of reciprocal retaliation might suffice to motivate a good deal of moral behavior in politics.

---

3 At least it should have this effect under the conditions of constantly shifting political alliances elaborated later in this chapter – which are, to some greater or lesser extent, sociologically and politically unrealistic just about everywhere in the world.

A mong those who would interpret extensions of the suffrage as being motivated by purely moral principles, much is made of the use of "consistency" arguments by advocates of extensions of the suffrage. It is wrong to withhold voting rights from women or blacks, it is said, for reasons that would not be taken as good grounds for withholding such rights from men. The inconsistency manifested by such dual standards is ordinarily taken as a powerful moral criticism of denying women or blacks the franchise on such grounds.

This theme figures especially largely in arguments for women's suffrage, for example.[4] "The reasons why women should vote are the same as the reasons why men should vote," one suffragette plainly stated.[5] No one says that the vote should be given to everyone: tests of age, sanity, criminality, and "stake in the community" have, at one time or another, been imposed. The essence of women's claim to the vote is simply that anyone who meets whatever general tests of that form that are imposed within her society should be entitled to vote and should not be debarred just because she is a woman. According to Helen Taylor's famous 1867 *Westminster Review* essay, "The Claim of Englishwomen to the Suffrage Constitutionally Considered" amounts to just this.[6]

The moral principle lying behind such arguments is, of course, the simple Golden Rule principle of universalization. Whatever grounds people give for extending or restricting the suffrage to one group of people, they ought – for the sake of consistency – to be prepared to apply the same grounds in

4 The demand that "women, too, must exercise 'the rights of men and citizens'" continues into our own day, albeit more hesitantly in light of the ambiguities in that claim to which post-modernism has sensitized us (Pateman 1990, p. 22).
5 Blackwell 1911, p. 1.
6 "Since women are permitted to hold property, they should also be permitted to exercise all the rights which, by our laws, the possession of property brings with it . . . ." – including the right to vote (Taylor 1867, p. 21). In similar vein, Lucrettia Mott asked rhetorically at the 1848 Rochester Woman's Rights Convention, "Does one man have fewer rights than another because his intellect is inferior? If not, why should woman?" (in Rochester Woman's Rights Convention 1848, p. 11); and the Senaca Falls "Declaration of Sentiments" of that same year likewise complains that man "has withheld from [woman] rights which are given to the most ignorant and degraded men – both natives and foreigners" (Seneca Falls Woman's Rights Convention 1848, p. 6).

deciding whether to extend or restrict the suffrage to any other group. If they are not, then there has to be some other, additional qualification that they are employing. And if it is just the brute fact of race or sex, *simpliciter*, then that provides no reason at all for denying them the vote when otherwise identical white males are granted it.

"Whence . . . comes this exception?" Helen Taylor asks.[7] "Why, when they possess the necessary property, are women, alone among citizens of full age and sane mind, unconvicted of crime, disabled by a merely personal circumstance (that of sex) from exercising a right attached by our institutions to property and not to persons?" The Premier of New Zealand, interviewed by an American suffragette in 1911, remarked that "a proposal to establish a sex line in politics would now be laughed at, and to the majority of the people of New Zealand the disenfranchisement of one-half of the population because they are women, would appear as ridiculous and as arbitrary as to withhold votes from a section of the men – say those with red hair."[8]

7 Taylor 1867, p. 30.
8 Sir Joseph George Ward (quoted in NAWSA 1971). The classic reply is that the law withholds the vote from those who are "dependent" upon others. It is a curious case of circular legal reasoning, though, when the only reason that people are thus dependent is that labor or matrimonial property law makes them so (Mill 1869; Titmuss 1958a). And besides, it is unclear why the sheer fact of dependency should be electorally disqualifying. Some, such as Mill (1861, chap. 8, p. 280), complain that letting recipients of poor relief vote invites them to put their hands into others' pockets; but that would be a justification for disqualifying any but the very richest from voting, since from Aristotle forward it has standardly been said that democracy is a system of exploitation of the rich few by the many poor. Others complain that dependents lack a will of their own. It is almost never literally true that they do not have a will of their own, though: the very young and very old are not lacking in wilfulness, whatever else they may lack, as anyone charged with their care can testify. What dependents arguably lack is, instead, independence of will. It is this sense in which Blackstone (1765, bk 1, chap. 2, sect. 5, pt 1, p. 165) and the American Founders following him (Guv. Morris, in Madison 1787, 7 August 1787, pp. 402–3) complain that giving dependents the suffrage amounts to double-counting the votes of those upon whom they are dependent: dependents will (or will be made to) vote the same way as those upon whom they depend. But the secret ballot should take care of that. Furthermore, if the interests of wives point in the same direction as those of their husbands, for example, those interests should count twice: there are, after all, two people whose interests point in that direction (Blackwell 1911, p. 2).

How much motivational (as opposed to purely moral) bite this argument might have is an open question. Those keen upon extending the suffrage count heavily upon it, standardly forming coalitions for systematic extension of the franchise right across the board. Thus, the ex-slave abolitionist leader Frederick Douglass spoke at the 1848 Rochester Women's Rights Convention, saying that "he should not dare claim a right that he would not concede to woman";[9] and women's rights campaigners were similarly active in the abolitionist movement.[10] The hope was that if any of them won all of them would win – both in the sense that if the argument was won for one group it would be won for all, and also in the sense that if any one group got the vote they would use their new-found political power similarly to further others' causes in seeking the suffrage.

A parallel example occurred in connection with the Reform Act of 1832, introducing a limited dose of democracy into the British House of Commons. Upon the eve of its enactment, a periodical styling itself the *Poor Man's Guardian* editorialized that "we cannot think so ill of human nature as to think that those who will . . . have gained their own freedom will not aid us to gain ours." Subsequent events proved them wrong.

> The poachers were successfully transformed into game-keepers. . . . Middle-class people, once given the vote, wanted to conserve institutions which they had formerly been inclined to attack. . . . Most of the new voters wanted, not to challenge the aristocracy, but to win recognition from it: once they had their rightful position they did not favour further adventures.[11]

In short, the moralizing constraints of consistency did not prove neccessarily motivationally binding upon those demanding expansions of the franchise for themselves but not necessarily for others.

Such examples serve to show that it is perfectly possible,

9   In Rochester Woman's Rights Convention 1848, p. 6.
10 See generally Tyler 1944, pt 3.
11 Brock 1973, pp. 315, 319. Indeed, advocates of the 1832 reform – Lord Grey and Lord John Russell among them – gave firm assurances that ministers regarded it as a "final" measure rather than as a first step toward further reforms (Hirschman 1991, pp. 93–4).

motivationally – even if it is perfectly impermissible, morally and even logically – for people to refuse to apply to others arguments that they would seek to employ in securing the vote for themselves. What we therefore need is a more nuanced examination of the way arguments offered for and against extensions of the franchise have actually worked in political discourse. We need to see whether it really was philosophical argument – arguments of morality and of logical consistency – that proved motivationally most compelling. Might there not have been a substantial element of pure reciprocity working at one remove?

The speculation lying behind that question is just this. Suppose we regard electoral-cum-parliamentary politics as an arena within which larger social conflicts are played out. Suppose, furthermore, they are "played out" there, quite literally: politics functions as a stage on which those conflicts could be acted out, in a way that mirrors more-or-less faithfully the way they would be played out in real life, only in a far less costly fashion.

If that is the function ascribed to formal politics, then it is obviously essential for all the key players to possess power within the political game proportional to the power that they possess outside it. That is the only way in which politics can hope to serve the conflict-mirroring, conflict-defusing role assigned to it, on that model. The political shadow-play can supplant actual social conflict, in this way, only if the outcomes of the one faithfully mirrors the most likely outcomes of the other. And that can be the case only if the power balances within the political arena faithfully mirror those within the broader social arena.

Extensions – and indeed contractions – of the franchise, more generally, are often analyzed in just such terms. As one Member of Parliament put it, in debates over woman's suffrage, "Votes are to swords exactly what bank notes are to gold – the one is effective only because the other is believed to be behind it . . . ."[12] By such reasoning it might be thought that

12 F. E. Smith, in a 1910 House of Commons debate. In a 1932 lecture, Harold Laski similarly held that "privilege never retreats until the purpose of its retreat has already been won." Both are quoted in Harrison (1978, p. 16).

extensions of the suffrage to women in 1918 and 1928 "merely registered at law a social change which was already complete."[13]

One of the most distinguished analysts of Southern politics in the United States says much the same. Post-Reconstruction laws disenfranchising blacks, V. O. Key claims, merely "recorded a *fait accompli* brought about, or destined to be brought about, by more fundamental political processes" anyway. The fate of the blacks was "signed and sealed" before the electoral laws were ever changed, and indeed those laws could only have been changed once the "more fundamental political processes" had already played themselves out.[14]

Or, again, we might imagine a stylized version of an ethnically "divided society," such that one group controls all the society's capital and the other all the society's labor. Since neither acting alone can produce anything at all, each in effect has an absolute economic veto over production. And if we are trying to supplant costly economic conflict with parallel political shadow-boxing, the political structure employed for the purpose must give to each party an analogous right of veto. The reason for giving each side a veto, politically, in such societies is merely that they already have one economically.[15]

Such examples are not limited to special cases of ethnically divided societies, though. Institutions such as weighted suffrage, plural votes, institutionalized sectional vetoes – now quaint, perhaps – have historically been found in some very

13   Cf. Harrison 1978, p. 16.
14   Key 1949, p. 533, 535. Kirchheimer (1969, p. 47) puts the point more generally: "in a democratic state, universal suffrage will not by and of itself bring about political decisions for which the way has not been paved by the will of the various groups. Even the freest electoral system can only support a preexisting political will . . . ."
15   Rogowski 1974, chap 4; something similar is involved in many of the cases of consociationalism discussed by Lijphart (1977). Sectoral divisions have, historically, played the same role in expanding the franchise: "Seigneurial and royal authorities, eager to gain control over the lucrative islands of capitalism to which they had previously granted charters, endeavored to ally with the lower classes to overthrow oligarchic rule. Burghers typically thwarted this movement by themselves extending rights thereby coopting outside entreaties. . . . [Or, again,] the free-trade patriciate and the vulnerable guilds eventually came into conflict over representation in government and protectionism. Overt conflict was often precluded by the two parties . . . negotiating charters that extended . . . citizenship rights" (Downing 1989, p. 224).

familiar places. In the old Austrian *Kurien* or Prussian three-class system "universal suffrage [is] granted, but the weights of the votes given to the lower classes are infinitesimal in comparison with those of the established landed or financial elite"; and in that way economic power-holders are ensured analogous political power as well.[16] In the United States, giving all states equal representation in a Senate with legislative authority coequal to that of the popularly-apportioned House of Representatives was originally conceived to be a device to ensure the slave states of the South an effective veto on national legislation.[17] All of those, though, seem to be devices for disenfranchising (in whole or in part) the masses, rather than of ensuring equal respect for the position of each person.

In the history of expanding the franchise, it is military rather than economic necessity which has most often proven decisive. Time and again, we are told that the suffrage has been or should be extended for war-related reasons.[18] Extending the franchise has long been regarded as one good way to encourage the previously disenfranchised to fight for their country or to take the place, economically, of those who have gone to fight. More often than not, extensions of the franchise come only after the fighting is over, as a form of moral "reward" for services rendered. But there is a forward-looking aspect to the act as well: those we once needed we are likely to need again.

Often this is put as a matter of high-minded principle. John Stuart Mill's *Representative Government* makes it a matter of justice that, "If [a person] is compelled to pay [taxes], if he may be compelled to fight, if he is required implicitly to obey, he should be legally entitled to be told what for; to have his consent asked, and his opinion counted . . . ."[19]

Such moralized appeals are not confined to philosophers alone, however. Many practical political appeals have been cast in just such high-minded terms, often with considerable

16 Bendix and Rokkan 1964, p. 99.
17 Thus rendering largely redundant Calhoun's (1853) argument for further institutionalizing the veto rights of a "concurrent majority."
18 "In a number of countries the demands for universal manhood suffrage became intimately tied in with the need for universal *conscription*. . . . In the Swedish suffrage debates, the slogan 'one man, one vote, one gun' reflects this tie up between franchise and military recruitment" (Bendix and Rokkan 1964, p. 94, n. 56).
19 Mill 1861, chap. 8, p. 277.

effect. Consider this incident, occurring shortly after the American Revolution. During the next election,

> an attempt was made . . . to turn away from the polls a
> group of young soldiers . . . .. One soldier retorted that the
> government had had no objections to their fighting "and
> now you have to our voting. This is not just; we have
> fought for the right of voting and we will now exercise it."

The observer reported, "It was not possible to reply to such an argument. The soldiers voted . . . ."[20] Nor is it fighting men alone who might benefit from such appeals. War workers – especially women and blacks – have, over the years, appealed with considerable success to precisely such principles to justify extending the postwar franchise to them as well.[21]

The argument from justice is not the only one available to warriors and war-workers, however. There is an argument from prudence as well. Those who have needed their services in the past are likely to need them in the future.[22] Seen in this light, rewards for past services become bribes for future ones. On this account, less typical is the example of the Grand Army of the Republic – marches by civil war pensioners flexing their political muscles when they manifestly no longer have any

20   Williamson 1960, p. 133. Similarly, in 1791 some lessees of Indian lands in South Carolina "petitioned the legislature for the right to vote inasmuch as they had 'fought for the Cause of Liberty'" (Ibid., p. 132); and an 1802 editorial of the *Fredericktown Hornet* demanded to know, "Who stood in the ranks as soldiers and fought the battles of the revolutuionary war? Is not the poor man now bound to do military duty? And do not the farmers and mechanics now fill the ranks of the militia companies? The soldier is as much entitled to vote as the Captain of the company or the Colonel of the regiment'" (quoted in Ibid., p. 147).

21   In the judgment of one of the most distinguished commentators on these events, the argument that "the war work done . . . by women . . . should be rewarded by enfranchising [them] . . . was the argument which, in so far as argument was important, did more than any other to win women the vote" in Britain during the First World War (Harrison 1978, p. 38; see more generally chap. 10).

22   Such arguments from prudence prove most compelling when the need for loyal troops is felt most acutely. Thus, for example, "In the wake of the [American] war scare of 1798, the argument was used that men good enough to fight were good enough to vote, with customary effect" (Williamson 1960, p. 147).

military muscle. More typical is the example of the medieval "village hundreds" in Scandinavia, where members arrived at the assembly with their weapons in hand and voted by raising their spears.[23]

This point was put with great clarity by Benjamin Franklin, speaking in favor of an extensive suffrage during the 1787 American Constitutional Convention. He recalled with pride the example of American sailors who, when captured, refused to turn coat and serve their British captors in a way that British sailors often did when captured by American vessels. And "this proceed[s]," Franklin suggests, "from the different manner in which the common people were treated in America and Great Britain."[24] The lesson, he thought, was clear: if we want loyal troops in the future, we have to treat people right in the present. It is not, or not merely, a matter of morality. It is also, at least in part, a matter of pure prudence.

A lexis de Tocqueville observes that, "Once a people begins to interfere with the voting qualification, one can be sure that sooner or later it will abolish it altogether," and he goes on to remark that "that is one of the most invariable rules of social behavior."[25] Like all ironclad generalizations in social science, that one is not invariably correct. "The French threw away universal suffrage after the Reign of Terror," for example.[26] But exceptions like that rather tend to prove the rule.

Elsewhere, the rule of an ever-expanding and never-contracting suffrage seems to hold broadly true. And unlike so many putative "laws" of politics, this one works through the conscious intentions of political actors rather than behind their backs. In various countries at various times, statesmen contemplating questions of the franchise have concluded that they quite simply could not disenfranchise those who were already enjoying the right to vote.

23 Downing 1989, p. 219.
24 Debate of 7 August 1787; quoted in Madison 1787, p. 404. The lesson that Franklin there draws from this anecdote is that "it is of great consequence that we should not depress the virtue and public spirit of our common people, of which they displayed a great deal during the [American Revolutionary] war, and which contributed principally to the favorable issue of it."
25 Tocqueville 1835, vol. 1, pt 1, chap. 4, pp. 52–3.
26 Maine 1885, essay 1.

In the US Constitution, for example, it is left to the respective states to determine qualifications for electors, even for national office. *The Federalist* explains, lamely, that "to have reduced the different qualifications in the different States to one uniform rule would probably have been . . . dissatisfactory to some of the States."[27] But as Madison's notes on the debates in the drafting convention makes plain, the real reason was the perceived political impossibility of disenfranchising people for national elections who were already entitled to vote in state elections.[28] The vote, once granted, cannot be taken away.

Or, for another example, consider how disparities between the suffrage requirements of different colonies were handled upon formation of the federated Commonwealth of Australia. "The Federal Parliament . . . had to make its own electoral laws," the wife of the speaker of the Australian House of Representatives recalled, in conversation with American suffragettes in 1911. "And to establish uniformity [it] was obliged to adopt the broadest existing basis, because the constitution forbade the outrage and anomaly of disenfranchising persons by whom some of its members had been elected."[29]

The general pattern is, then, clear enough. What we see is ever-expanding and (almost) never-contracting voting rights. The question is how to explain such a pattern. The explanation that Tocqueville himself offered was purely in terms of political pressures:

27   Madison, in Hamilton, Madison, and Jay 1788, no. 52.
28   In the notes on the debate of 7 August 1787, for example, Madison (1787, pp. 401–2) records Colonel Mason as remarking that "eight or nine States have extended the right of suffrage beyond the mere freeholders," and asking, "what will the people there say, if they should be disenfranchied" by a less generous provision in the Federal Constitution; and Mr Butler concurred, "There is no right of which the people are more jealous than that of suffrage."
29   Quoted in NAWSA 1971. Actually, all that Section 41 of Constitution of the Commonwealth of Australia requires is that: "No adult person who has or acquires a right to vote at elections for the more numerous House of the Parliament of a State shall, while the right continues, be prevented by any law of the Commonwealth from voting at elections for either House of the Parliament of the Commonwealth" (Sawer 1988, p. 45). But the Speaker's wife's report of the popular perception, both of that requirement and of its underlying logic, is more important in the present context than the dry constitutional facts of the matter.

The further . . . voting rights [are] extended, the stronger is the need felt to spread them still wider; for after each new concession the forces of democracy are strengthened, and its demands increase with its augmented power. The ambition of those left below the qualifying limit increases in proportion to the number of those above it. Finally the exception becomes the rule; concessions follow one another without interruption, and there is no halting place until universal suffrage has been attained.[30]

The reference to the "forces for democracy" here seems to imply an assumption that people who had been arguing for an extension of the franchise before they had it would necessarily continue arguing for such extensions after they themselves achieved it. That assumption is false, in ways that have already been discussed.

What is nonetheless true – and what is subject to a straight-forwardly political explanation that will actually hold water – is this. No one who has the vote is prepared to see it lost without a fight. And in that fight, those votes themselves will feature as crucial weapons.

The vote is standardly seen as a bulwark against tyranny.[31] As such, it is never more needed than by those targeted to lose it – who, once having lost it, will presumably be targeted in like fashion for still more onerous burdens.[32] That fact gives

30 Tocqueville 1835, vol. 1, pt 1, chap. 4, pp. 52–3.
31 "Rulers and ruling classes are under a necessity of considering the interests and wishes of those who have the suffrage; but of those who are excluded, it is in their option whether to do so or not. . . . Men, as well as women, do not need political rights in order that they may govern, but in order that they may not be misgoverned" (Mill 1861, chap. 8, pp. 277, 291). In American discussions of voting rights for blacks, for example, the proposition that "'A voteless people is a hopeless people,' has become a cliche. . . . Former Attorney General William P. Rogers once stated that, 'The right to vote occupies a key position because it provides means of protecting other rights. When minority groups exercise their franchise more effectively, it almost invariably follows that they achieve a greater measure of other fundamental freedoms'" (Keech 1968, p. 2).
32 Thus, Benjamin Franklin commented in the debates in the Federal Convention on 7 August 1787 that "he did not think that the elected had any right . . . to narrow the privileges of the electors. He quoted as arbitrary the "British Statute . . . narrowing the right of suffrage to persons having freeholds of a certain value; observing that this Statue

those due to lose the vote a motive for resisting contractions in the suffrage. And the fact that they presently have the vote gives them the political power (or anyway a political resource) with which to prosecute that campaign.

There may, in fact, be no good explanation – or anyway no general one – as to why the suffrage is ever expanded. Each extension of the suffrage might be an *ad hoc* response to the political urgencies of the moment: someone needs someone's help, and conceding them the suffrage is the price that they pay to get it.[33] In a way, though, that does not much matter. All that is required is a systematic barrier, on the other side, against contractions in the franchise. So long as those barriers are firmly in place, then the episodic extensions of the suffrage consequent upon accidents of history will never be reversed, and the long-run tendency will be for the suffrage always to expand and never to contract.[34] And that systematic tendency for the suffrage sometimes to expand and never to contract can be explained purely in terms of power politics and people using their votes to protect their own interests.

Models of reciprocity in the moral realm are reflected, in the political realm, in the workings of the franchise. It is the threat of the reciprocal use of the franchise that dissuades citizens from trying to oppress one another too badly: what you and your coalition do to us today, we and our coalition may well be able to do to you tomorrow. And it is the episodic need for others' reciprocal assistance, in turn, that explains the award of the franchise in the first place.

The politics of the franchise thus go far toward explaining

---

was soon followed by another under the succeeding Parliament, subjecting the people who had no votes to peculiar labors and hardships" (quoted in Madison 1787, p. 404).

33   "Universal suffrage . . . was twice revived in France, that the Napoleonic tyranny might be founded on it; and it was introduced into Germany, that the personal power of Prince Bismarck might be confirmed" (Maine 1885, essay 1). As Kirchheimer (1969, p. 44 n) comments on the latter case, "Universal suffrage, introduced as a weapon of the conservative government against . . . the propertied bourgeoisie, turned into a promotional platform of a proletariat which had become self sufficient." Cf. Bendix and Rokkan 1964, p. 94.

34   A similar analysis of the ever-expanding number of government agencies is offered in Kaufman 1976.

basic political decency in terms of sheer reciprocity. The vote will be enjoyed by any class of people whom others have ever needed. Everyone who has the vote can, through the threat of reciprocal retaliation using it, make reasonably certain that others will not exploit them – politically, at least – too badly.

But with franchise politics, as with models of reciprocity more generally, such protections work only insofar as retaliation is a serious threat. There are some who are and who for the conceivable future will remain winners, while others will for the conceivable future remain losers. And, cruel though it may be to say so, perpetual losers are politically of no account.[35]

Insofar as there are some who politically really are perpetual losers, their threats of reciprocal retaliation – electorally, as otherwise – can hardly be expected to move people. Or at least they cannot absent some other argument, infusing for example a deeper form of uncertainty into political machinations. It is that to which the next chapter turns.

35 The cruelty is manifest. Consider the compelling tale told by Wasserstrom (1964, p. 641) of "a lengthy account in a Southern newspaper about the high school band program in a certain city. The article described fully the magnificence of the program and emphasized especially the fact that it was a program in which *all high school students* in the city participated. Negro children neither were nor could be partipants in the program. The article, however, saw no need to point that out. I submit that it neglected to do so not because everyone knew the fact, but because in a real sense the writer and the newspaper do not regard Negro high school students as children – persons, human beings – at all." The effect "is to read certain persons . . . out of the human race. . . . What is the negro parent who reads this article to say to his children? What are his children supposed to think? How does a Negro parent even begin to demonstrate to the world that his children are really children, too? These are burdens no civilized society ought ever to impose." As Mill (1861, chap. 8, p. 283) puts it, "Every one has a right to feel insulted by being made a nobody, and stamped as of no account at all."

SIX

Entrenched Rights and Constitutional Constraints

The whole point of constitutions, as contemporarily conceived, is to constrain the arbitrary will of rulers.[1] Constitutions, by their nature, regularize the exercise of political power and circumscribe the prerogatives of the sovereign. On medieval understandings, that amounted principally to protecting "the people" (mostly the feudal barons) against the monarch. On modern understandings, that amounts particularly to protecting minorities from the exercise of the sovereign will of majorities.[2]

Constitutions are essentially "power maps."[3] They first and foremost "constitute" the political organization of the community. In the very act of constituting it, they to some extent necessarily constrain it: there are certain things that political institutions, constituted in any particular way, simply cannot do. Additional constraints are imposed, and further protections afforded, through lists of "entrenched rights" incorporated into that basic law itself. Any constitution which failed to secure people's liberties in some such way arguably does not qualify as a constitution "proper" at all: it would be a constitution in name only, merely a façade.[4]

1 Classical understandings differed. But "the principle of . . . limitations upon power and authority was a fundamental constitutional principle underlying the new system of canon law" from the eleventh century onwards (Berman 1983, p. 215).
2 McIlwain 1947. Friedrich 1968; 1974. Downing 1989. Maddox 1989.
3 Duchacek 1973. Sartori 1962.
4 Sartori (1962, p. 861) distinguishes on precisely these grounds between

Entrenched rights take many forms. They might be substantive (rights to freedom of property, speech, religion and association) or procedural (ranging from guarantees of "due process of law" to giving minorities an explicit veto over policy[5]). Entrenched rights may bolster the powers of minorities (ensuring them certain protections and prerogatives) or undercut the powers of others to do things to harm them (outlawing private armies or secret societies, for example[6]). Entrenched rights may be positive (rights *to* welfare, *to* work, *to* strike) or negative (rights to be free *from* the interference of others, in various respects).[7] In all these ways and more, there is great variation in what the contents of entrenched rights are, when they come into operation, with what effect, and for what purpose.[8]

Whatever precise form they take, however, the whole point of constitutionalizing rights is undoubtedly to "entrench" them.[9] Being thus embodied in a hard-to-change-constitution

---

"constitutions proper" (*garantiste* constitutions), "nominalist" constitutions and façade (or "fake" or "trap") constitutions.

5   The standard mechanism is through separate chambers. Perhaps the most dramatic example – because politically the most implausible – is Calhoun's (1853) proposal for making legislation subject to approval by a "concurrent majority" of slaveholding classes.

6   Examples, admittedly legislative rather than constitutional in character, include: in Great Britain, the Unlawful Oath Act of 1797, Seditious Meetings Act of 1817 and Unlawful Societies Acts of 1799; in France, Article 291 of the Code Pénal of 1788; in Germany, sects 128, 129 of the Criminal Code of 15 May 1871 (Lowenstein 1938, pp. 600–1). Consider similarly "blouse laws" prohibiting "indoctrinary haberdashery" – the wearing of paramilitary costumes and, especially, the carrying of firearms by civilians (Ibid. p. 725).

7   Spiro 1959, pp. 405–6.

8   Waldron (1988) insightfully characterizes rights in general as *in extremis* arrangements: as minima rather than maxima; as specifying fallback arrangements for what to do when other more affective bonds of community have broken down, rather than as descriptions of how we would most like to live our collective lives.

9   Here I focus upon the purely practical side of rights guarantees. In addition to these practical protections there are, however, important symbolic functions served by rights guarantees. In particular, rights guarantees are crucial in protecting the dignity and self-respect of people. This point is made, in abstract terms, in Feinberg (1980, chap. 7) and Goodin (1982, chap. 5); for a particularly evocative example, see Wasserstrom's (1964, p. 641) discussion of how an established system of human rights might have protected Southern blacks against affronts so profound as to constitute an "intolerable burden."

makes them far more secure than similar protections would have been, had they been mere creatures of ordinary legislation.[10] That fact is so familiar with respect to classical constitutional rights that its force may well be missed. To drive it home, let us focus instead upon another example from a less familiar domain: the proposal to embed a right to an old-age pension in the American Constitution itself.

One Yale professor reports himself "constantly astonished by the number of my students who, when asked, assert . . . that they will not get Social Security" – adding that, tellingly, "there seems to be no comparable skepticism about whether bonds and treasury notes will be repaid."[11] Much of the peculiar political pathology surrounding old age pensions arguably derives from this perceived insecurity of those entitlements.

The obvious solution to such a problem, and to the politico-economic pathology that flows from it, is for social security entitlements to be formally incorporated into the US Constitution itself. "Constitutionalizing" social security in this way provides a "fabric of confidence."[12] After all, constitutions cannot be changed nearly so casually as mere legislative enactments themselves. So there would then be no need to treat every alteration to benefit structures and levels as the "thin end of the wedge" that will end up destroying social security altogether.

There is nothing surprising or, presumably, exceptionable in any of this. The most standard way in which constitutions perform their familiar function of preventing the abuse of power and of protecting minorities is by embodying rights and rules in a document that stands above, and endures beyond, ordinary political machinations.

How exactly constitutions work to accomplish that goal remains largely unanalyzed, however. Why do people write

10   This feature figures largely in discussions of "inalienable, natural rights." According to what is perhaps the most persuasive account, what is "inalienable" is not any particular right itself but rather institutions to protect rights (Brown 1955): that much, at the very least, is not subject to ordinary political horse-trading.

11   Cover 1988, p. 82.

12   The hope is that "at some point someone might say of Social Security, as one might say of a treasury note, 'I am not sure whether the return is quite adequate, but I know it is safe'" (Ibid. pp. 83).

constitutions? And why do they continue to respect them, even after the original constellation of interests and powers giving rise to them has shifted? If would-be oppressors have the numbers which would be politically required to oppress some group within the community, why do they let constitutional constraints stand in their way? Told that a measure that he advocated was unconstitutional, one Southern Senator replied, "When the Constitution comes between me and the virtue of the white women of South Carolina, I say: To hell with the Constitution."[13] Why do not more people say likewise?

I shall here be suggesting that the answer lies, in large measure, in a motivational shift. There are, I suggest, some special features of thinking in terms of political constitutions (and of the basic institutions of society, more generally) that evoke different and morally superior responses from people.

In a way, that claim, too, is unsurprising. We are quite accustomed to constitutional questions being addressed in elevated – indeed, stilted – tones.[14] But we are inclined to suppose that that is just so much puffery. We are inclined to suppose that people just think it somehow more "appropriate," in discussions of higher law, to appeal to higher moral principles and to employ loftier rhetoric. That may well be part of the story. But I would argue that there is another side to it as well.

---

13 Quoted in Friedrich 1968, p. 123.
14 In *The Federalist*, for example, James Madison writes, "The [1787 US Constitutional] Convention . . . enjoyed, in a very singular degree, an exemption from the pestilential influence of party animosities; the diseases most incident to deliberative bodies, and most apt to contaminate their proceedings. [Furthermore] . . . all the deputations composing the Convention, were either satisfactorily accommodated by the final act; or were induced to accede to it, by a deep conviction of the necessity of sacrificing private opinions and partial interests to the public good. . . ." (Hamilton, Madison, and Jay 1788, no. 37, pp. 238–9). We might be tempted to take that with a grain of salt, since the *Federalist* papers were after all intended as promotional pamphlets. But it is noteworthy that similar comments recur in the preface to Madison's notes on Federal convention, not intended for publication in his lifetime. There Madison (1787, p. 19) writes "that there never was an assembly of men, charged with a great and arduous trust, who were more pure in their motives, or more exclusively or anxiously devoted to the object committed to them, than were the members of the Federal Convention of 1787, to the object of devising and proposing a constitutional system which would best supply the defects of that which it was to replace, and best secure the permanent liberty and happiness of their country."

What I would emphasize about constitutional deliberations is just this. When asked to choose fundamental laws and basic structures for their society, people are perforce contemplating schemes designed to persist into the indefinite future; when doing so, they are forced to extend their time horizons, thinking in terms of further futures than they would ordinarily have any reason to contemplate; and the further into the future they project their deliberations, the greater will be the uncertainties surrounding their own fate.[15] I have argued in chapter 3 that the greater the uncertainty the greater the consequent impartiality with which even the most purely prudential actor will be forced to reflect upon the possible plights of all people in general.

This is not the ordinary way in which constitutionalism is viewed, to be sure.[16] But it is not without precedent, either. One such is Hume's argument for settled rules of justice, a self-imposed restraint upon people's myopic time preferences. The rule of law, according to Hume, is a device by which people force themselves to give due regard to their long-term interests in face of temptations to pursue present advantage.[17]

15   And, it might be added, the fates of those near and dear to them – most especially, in this context, their children. Appealing to the possible plight of one's progeny is a common device – among both political philosophers (e.g., Rawls 1971, sect. 22) and constitutional framers alike – for encouraging people to take a more impartial concern with the plight of all. At the American Constitutional Convention of 1787, for example, George Mason reminded delegates that "however affluent their circumstances, or elevated their situations might be, the course of a few years not only might but certainly would distribute their posterity throughout the lowest classes of Society. Every selfish motive . . ., every family attachment, ought [therefore] to recommend such a system of policy as would provide no less carefully for the rights and happiness of the lowest than of the highest orders of Citizens" (quoted in Madison 1787, notes for 31 May, p. 40). Without denying either the ethical validity or practical importance of such appeals, I shall here focus upon the purer case of how to appeal to pure egoists. Whatever can be said to induce them to behave well can apply, *mutatis mutandis*, to people who are partial altruists who want also to advance the interests of particular others (their offspring, and perhaps their offsprings' offspring) if not everyone in general.

16   For more standard accounts, see the various papers in Pennock and Chapman 1979, for example.

17   Hume (1739, bk 3, pt 2, sect. 7) puts it this way: "when we consider any objects at a distance, all their minute distinctions vanish, and we always give the preference to whatever is in itself preferable. . . . But on my

Another precedent is to be found in Rawls's grounds for focusing upon "the basic structure" of society as the proper subject of a theory of justice. The argument he gives for that focus is that asking people to frame long-lived institutions, with all the attendant uncertainties, might force them to reflect almost as impartially as they would under his "veil of ignorance."[18] Although non-standard, my approach is not without precedent, then.

This analysis dovetails nicely with my earlier argument about how uncertainty in general might make people behave more morally than they would otherwise have done. The emphasis in chapter 3 was upon the brute sociological facts: even over the fairly short term, people's fates were much more fluid than they ever imagined. The emphasis here is upon socio-political devices to further increase those uncertainties, by extending the time horizon which is relevant to people in judging the issues before them.

Not only is it uncertainty which, on the account that I shall offer, serves to make constitutional deliberations morally special. So too, it might be argued, is it uncertainty that makes democratic deliberations themselves morally special. Furthermore, it is arguably merely the failure of uncertainty at the level of democratic deliberations which makes recourse to the constitutional level of discourse necessary at all.

Let us begin this argument where the last chapter left off. The problem there in view, recall, lay in supplying purely prudential political actors with a motive for not exploiting people who cannot mount a credible threat of reciprocal retaliation – people who are in no position to help or to harm them.

For such a threat to be credible, though, we need not be

---

nearer approach, . . . a new inclination to the present good springs up, and makes it difficult for me to adhere inflexibly to my first purpose and resolution. This natural infirmity I may very much regret, and I may endeavour, by all possible means, to free my self from it." Recognizing how "ineffectual" private remedies are, we will on Hume's account be led to "embrace with pleasure" rules of justice and magistrates to enforce them as an "expedient, by which I may impose a restraint upon myself, and guard against this weakness."

18   Rawls 1977.

absolutely certain that it will be carried out. Complete uncertainty might be almost as good for these purposes. It might be sufficiently threatening simply to be able to say, "You cannot count on being in your privileged position forever; there is every reason to suppose that I shall someday be in a position to do unto you what you do unto me today."

Some such thought arguably is precisely what underlies key arguments in favor of majoritarian democracy itself. What drives one particularly compelling version of that argument is essentially an assumption of complete uncertainty – uncertainty about how many allies you will have, and who they will be, on any given occasion. In effect, you are asked to assume that you cannot count on any "standing arrangements" to deliver you the votes of any fixed number of allies on any given occasion; any given person is as likely to be with you as against you on any given occasion. If that assumption is granted, then an elegant mathematical result straightforwardly follows. Majority rule can then be proven to be the decision rule which uniquely maximizes the sum of each person's wins less his or her losses over the long haul.[19]

The moral importance of this result is clear enough. Uncertainty would in that case have forced even political egoists to accept, as a matter of pure prudence, a procedure which impartially reflects the preferences of everyone. The preferences of each person are weighed equally and options are chosen just according to how many people favor them.[20]

Furthermore, in this sort of world uncertainty would provide

19   Taylor (1969) proves the proposition, based on earlier speculation and partial formalization by Rae (1969).

20   May's (1952) remarkable proof is of particular interest here. In effect, it says that if we want impartiality, both as between people (no one's vote counts for more than one) and as between positions (no alternative wins just because it is the *status quo*), then we are committed to majority rule. Technically, the proof establishes that these two conditions plus two others constitute necessary and sufficient conditions for majority rule to be the social decision rule. But those other conditions are little more than what is required for a rule to operate as a decision rule at all. They just demand that the rule always yield a decision, even if it is only a tie; and that in case of a tie, should one person switch his or her vote then the outcome will be whichever option he or she switches to. Clearly, the interest in the proof lies not with those innocuous conditions, but rather with the tight link it forges between majority rule and impartiality of the previously specified sorts.

majorities with a powerful reason for practicing characteristically liberal kinds of self-restraint in the exercise of their powers. In a world of complete political uncertainty, each person is as likely to win as they are to lose on any given occasion. Each would, therefore, have a powerful motive for refraining from imposing upon others any burdens that they would themselves find onerous, should others come to power and impose analogous burdens upon them. The unpredictable and shifting political alliances which serve as the defining feature of electoral uncertainty virtually guarantee regular alternation in power, or at least the *ex ante* expectation of it. And the prospect of such power shifts restrains people in the exercise of power which only temporarily resides with them.

All proofs of these propositions, however, hinge crucially on the assumption that there are no "standing arrangements" (no "permanent factions") in your society. For those proofs, it has to be assumed that any given person is as likely to vote with you as against you on any given occasion. In Aristotle's famous phrase, it has to be the case (or at least it has to be expected to be the case, *ex ante*) that everyone will "rule and be ruled, in turn."[21] Absent some such assumption, there is no reason to suppose that majoritarian procedures work out to everyone's long-term advantage. The proof just does not go through.

Politically, of course, that assumption is a highly unrealistic one. In most societies there are standing factions. Furthermore, those factions are usually far from ephemeral, enduring for some considerable time. People do know, broadly speaking, who their political friends and foes will be. The cast does not change all that dramatically from one moment to the next.

Insofar as the veil of uncertainty is lifted in that way, so too is the rationale for impartiality that is predicated upon it. Politically just as economically, the more confident you can be of winning the less reason you have for being solicitous of the interests of those who find themselves on the losing side. Where there are stable factions, some will be regular winners

---

21 Any other procedure with the same effect – rotation in office combined with election by lot, in the context of classical Greece – would do as well. But among the small set of decision rules with that property, majoritarian democracy seems the only one remotely feasible, politically, in the contemporary world.

while others are perpetual losers.[22] Persistent minorities are, under majoritarian democratic rules, persistent losers. And persistent losers are politically of no account.

People in those sorts of position are, in terms of the political logic developed here, eminently exploitable. Extensive though the franchise may be, and democratic though our majoritarian principles may be in aggregating those votes, there is simply nothing for political majorities to fear from such persistent minority members of the polity.[23] The political analog of reciprocity does nothing to persuade the majority community to treat such persistent minorities fairly, because there is no real prospect that politically they will ever in our lifetimes be in a position to do unto us as we have done unto them. If we are to be persuaded to treat them fairly nonetheless, it must be to some principle beyond mere reciprocity and its political equivalents to which the appeal is being made.

That sets up the problem to which constitutionalism, as here conceived, constitutes a solution. The problem is a failure of uncertainty. Persistent minorities are left unprotected by the automatic operation of political reciprocity under majoritarian voting systems. The source of the problem is precisely that those minorities are persistent, composed of the same people time and again, without doubt and without variation.

The solution that constitutionalism offers is to make political institutions even more persistent. If we can succeed in making political institutions more durable than political cleavages, then that will in turn introduce a certain measure of doubt about likely outcomes of factional fights in the further future. You will then no longer be certain whether you will be among the majority or minority throughout the long life of a constitution – or indeed over any significant portion of it.

22   Blacks in the American South might once have been one example, Catholics in Ulster another – Rose (1976a) discusses the parallels between them.
23   Keech's (1968, pp. 108, 107) observations on *The Impact of Negro Voting* in the American South are apposite: "The prospects that votes will help eliminate basic inequalities in the life chances of Negroes are contingent on the degree to which appropriate programs fit within the value structure of elites and voting majorities. . . . Universal suffrage is perfectly consistent with a highly stratfied society . . . Durham [North Carolina] is an excellent example of this. . . . White voting majorities have prevailed consistently over Negro minorities . . . ."

That the futher future might be uncertain in such ways is plausible enough. Clearly, it is unrealistic to imagine, as mathematical proofs in defense of majority rule require us to do, that political alliances are constantly and completely in flux. But the opposite image – of completely persistent, never-changing majorities dominating completely persistent, never-changing minorities – is also too extreme. In a world of relatively stable factions, there might be little *immediate* threat of today's majority turning into tomorrow's minority. In the longer term, though, factions might always realign, with old dimensions of cleavage losing their significance and new ones gaining it. So even in a world of fairly stable factions, where majorities have little to fear in the short term, the more distant future might be surrounded by sufficient uncertainty to evoke a more impartial attitude even from those presently on top.

Constitutional constraints are the classic way of trying to evoke, politically, the uncertainties surrounding those more distant futures. By both nature and design, constitutions and the various other basic institutions of society are long-term arrangements. Drafters of constitutions are invariably sensitive to that fact. They go to great lengths to ensure that their handicraft endures.

Sometimes they try too hard. Constitutional draftsmen from the 1291 Swiss confederation to the 1787 American convention have seen themselves as drafting documents that will, "God willing, last eternally."[24] They attempt to ensure "immortality."[25] Sometimes they try too hard, concocting documents that are so rigid they end up being brittle.[26] Try as they might, though, even the best constitutional draftsmen cannot realistically expect to frame documents that will last, literally, forever. Literal immortality is as impossible for political artifacts as it is for natural individuals.

True though that may be, it is as unnecessary as it is impossible to frame constitutional rules of literally infinite

24 In the words of the 1291 Swiss agreement establishing the "First Eternal League" (quoted in Spiro 1959, p. 393). See similarly Madison 1787, notes for 29 June, p. 214.
25 Madison, in Hamilton, Madison, and Jay 1788, no. 38, p. 246.
26 Reflecting upon the "rigidity of French constitutions, . . . an English critic" – Dicey (1908, p. 474) – "smiles at the labour wasted in France on the attempt to make immutable Constitutions which, on an average, have lasted about ten years apiece."

duration. It is quite enough, for the purposes here in view, that they be of *indefinitely* long duration. Sufficient uncertainty to make people behave morally will have been engendered by ensuring that constitutions last a long time, just so long as no one knows precisely how long. The period need not be literally infinite. It need only be of long and unpredictable duration.[27]

While it is folly to suppose that we can set constitutional arrangements in concrete, fixing them once and for all time, there is no folly at all in trying to make constitutions awfully hard to change. It is a common feature of constitutional arrangements that, once in place, they are not easily altered. That is typically ensured by stipulating especially (but not impossibly) arduous procedures for their subsequent amendment, for example.[28] Special assemblies must be called. Amendments must pass by super-large majorities. They must be agreed by a number of different people over a number of different years. And so on.[29]

People looking for long-term assurances in the face of long-term uncertainties will, therefore, be particularly tempted to embrace constitutional mechanisms as the embodiments of them.[30] And the effect of such uncertainty, in the case of constitutional choice, is much the same as in other realms. It forces upon people a more impartial, and hence more moral, attitude.

The most mundane reason for people taking a more impartial attitude toward constitutional questions is just this. The same rules will remain in force over the long haul, during which time political, social, and economic alliances may well shift

27 Similarly, in the Prisoner's Dilemma game that is so often taken to underlie tit-for-tat rationality, it is not necessary to sustain tit-for-tat that there be infinite iterations of the same game between the same players; it is enough that there merely be an indefinite number of them, to prevent "backwards induction" from inducing everyone to refuse to cooperate from the start.

28 A few constitutions – among them the 1848 Italian Constitution, the present New Zealand Constitution, and even Bentham's proposed Constitutional Code – can be amended by ordinary legislative procedures (Grey 1979, p. 193). Even there, however, there will presumably be pretty powerful "norms" dictating that the constitution not be amended lightly.

29 Friedrich 1968, chap 8. Bryce (1901) traces a continuum of "rigidity" and "flexibility" in constitutions, according to how easily they are amended.

30 Buchanan 1987, pp. 1435–6. Brennan and Buchanan 1985.

dramatically. People are therefore forced to take a Golden Rule attitude toward matters of constitutional choice – opting for rules that they would be prepared to have applied to them, if they were in other people's positions – quite simply because, over the long haul, they may well be in those other people's positions at some time or another. In this way, the constitutional constraints and limited governments characteristic of liberal democracy might likewise be traced simply to the workings of uncertainty in the political realm, making people more moral than they might otherwise be inclined to be.

There is an incongruity here, nonetheless. The essence of the matter is just this. Constitutionalism makes people morally impartial, on my analysis, by appealing to considerations of what would be prudent for them to choose, were they making decisions about principles that would remain in force, in effect, "forever." But it does so under conditions in which it is, on the face of it, both prudentially unwise and practically unnecessary to cast principles in that "forevermore" form.

The further future is necessarily more uncertain. But why then should prudential agents go out of their way to try to fix rules to govern their dealings in those uncertain futures? The ordinary course for prudential agents, faced with substantial uncertainties, is to try to keep their options open. The greater the uncertainty, the greater their "liquidity preference," to borrow the language of high finance.

The incongruity is compounded by the fact that in settling rules governing their conduct in those uncertain further futures, people would necessarily have to adopt rules constraining their pursuit of private advantage in the shorter term, where the situation is not in the least uncertain. In terms of pure prudence, it is prima facie bizarre that people should renounce the pursuit of narrow self-interest, in circumstances in which they could be pursued with confidence and indeed impunity. It is all the more bizarre when they do so in order to settle something that need not – and prudentially ought not – be settled, just yet.

In a nutshell, why write constitutions which are hard to change when you could simply have written laws which are easy to change?[31] The answer would be obvious if you could

31 And, come to that, why cast rules in the form of laws and statutes that

thereby fix in place forever arrangements particularly advantageous to you. But that is not only unrealistic politically but impossible, practically, given that you are necessarily uncertain as to which arrangements actually would work to your peculiar advantage over the long haul. And the question of why write constitutions rather than ordinary laws or mere administrative edicts becomes all the more pressing, once we realize that the conditions of constitutional choice are such as to preclude people from pursuing as effectively as they otherwise might private advantage and narrow sectional self-interest.

Morally more worthy results are thereby achieved, to be sure. No doubt that is an important argument for constitutionalizing our politics. But if (or, rather, insofar as) that forms any part of agents" own motives for doing the one rather than the other, then to that extent constitutionalism does not *make* people moral. Instead, it merely *reflects* people's morality. It merely reflects the fact that they already are disposed toward behaving (or to forcing themselves to behave) morally. Constitutionalism then presents itself as no more than the chosen mechanism for manifesting people's pre-existing moral motives, rather than serving as an independent source of their motives for behaving in a morally impartial fashion, in the first place.

A constitution has been described as a "magic wall."[32] The key analytic question is how that magic might work. Why do people write constitutions? Having written them, why do they obey them?

Once there was an easy answer. The medieval natural-law formulation (which owes much to Roman antecedents, in turn) holds that even the king should be *sub deo et lege*.[33] There is a "higher," God-given law above which even an absolute sovereign must not put himself. All of us – the strong and the weak

---

require formal repeal, rather than letting much be settled according to case law made in courts or administrative agencies under your control (Kirchheimer 1969, pp. 428–52; Calabresi 1982). Statute law, too, can serve as a "frozen authoritative text" binding us even when our particular interests may have changed (Maley 1987).

32   Kirchheimer 1969, pp. 428–52.
33   McIlwain 1947, esp. chaps 3–4. Maddox 1989.

alike – should respect that higher law. That, on the natural-law understanding of constitutions, is why we should write constitutions. That, on the natural-law understanding, is why we should respect them.

All that made a fair bit of sense when the "higher law" in question was thought to derive from heavenly sources. The "higher law" tradition driving American constitutionalism, for example, was clearly of this sort. The "truths" to which Jefferson appealed as "self-evident" – the "inalienable rights" which his Declaration of Independence articulated – are fixed in the nature of the universe. Constitutions do not create such things, they merely reflect them.[34]

This way of thinking nowadays seems something of a relic. The last great exposition of this position, tooth and claw, is perhaps *The Laws of Eclesiastical Polity* by an author known to posterity (if at all) principally by Locke's allusion to "the judicious Hooker."[35] But in a more diffuse, underanalyzed sort of way, this manner of thinking about constitutions remains influential.[36] The present focus upon procedures merely masks what was once explicit, which is that higher law requries a higher warrant.[37]

So long as constitutions were regarded implicitly or explicitly

34 Corwin 1928–9. Consider the contemporaneous precedents. Lord Camden held in an 1766 opinion that taxation without representation is "absolutely illegal" under English law because it is "contrary to the fundamental laws of nature, contrary to the fundamental laws of this constitution . . . a constitution grounded on the eternal and immutable laws of nature" (quoted in Grey 1979, p. 203).
35 Hooker 1648; Locke 1690, sect. 5. See further Friedrich 1964.
36 The contemporary trick is to appeal to "natural laws" without going into too much detail about how exactly nature has ordained them, to appeal to "right reason" without going into too much detail about what exactly makes that particular form of reasoning right. The implicit claim, rarely cashed out, is that there can be some secular equivalent to God underwriting higher law and explaining why that higher law should prevail over lower. But that claim is – with honorable exceptions (e.g., Shue 1980) – typically left implicit.
37 Procedural principles like "no man be a judge in his own cause" – Coke's famous rule in *Dr Bonham's Case* (Corwin 1928–9) – might seem more "self-evident" and less in need of any higher warrant than substantive ones. To some extent these procedural principles really can be derived from what is required for a system of rules to function as a system of rules at all. But Lon Fuller (1969) tellingly dubs that the "lower law" rather than any form of "higher" law.

as embodiments of timeless truths with a transcendental warrant, it was clear enough why constitutional constraints should constrain. On a more purely secular understanding of the nature of constitutions, though, it is much more of an open question how and why constitutions constrain at all. If constitutions are purely human creations, then what humans have done humans ought, in principle, be able to undo.

The question of why and how constitutions constrain is really a pair of questions. One side of the issue concerns *how*, exactly, constitutions constrain: what are the mechanisms, and how and why do they work? A second side of the issue concerns *why*, exactly, people impose these constraints upon themselves: what are the motives for people imposing upon themselves constitutional constraints that deny them powers that they could otherwise exercise with impunity?

As I have already said, that latter question used to admit of an easy answer, in the days when people still subscribed to a frankly transcendental "natural law" understanding of what constitution-writing was all about. On that reading of the situation, it was not people who were imposing constraints upon themselves; rather, people were merely recognizing constraints imposed independently from above, by heavenly ordinance, natural law, and right reason. Their motive for obeying such ordinances was tied, in turn, to their motives for respecting those "higher" sources of that higher law, in the first place.

When we are seen merely to be imposing constraints upon ourselves, though, the question becomes more challenging. Suppose the effect of writing constitutions is indeed to force us to think further into the future than we would otherwise need to do, in ways that I have described. And suppose the effect of that, in turn, is to impose upon us a prudential motive for treating the interests of all with more impartial regard than we would otherwise have done. What *prudential* motive can we have for doing that?

Constitutionalism, I have argued, has the morally desirable effects it does by appealing to people's prudence, temporally extended. But pure prudence would surely lead the same people to resist any purely gratuitous extension of their time horizons. Purely prudent people do not court uncertainty needlessly. Yet that seems to be what they are doing in acceding to constitutional constraints running further into the future than they can foresee their interests lying.

One response might be that the extended time horizon and its moral consequences are altogether unintended, perhaps unwelcome but nonetheless inevitable corollaries of activities in which people need (or badly want) to engage for other purposes. For various other reasons, we need our institutions to be structured. We need for them to proceed according to regular, predictable patterns. We need a basic law, which we reliably know will persist in something like its present form into the indefinite future, in order to proceed about our own personal business in an orderly fashion.[38] And that necessary regularity in the basic law, in turn, imposes serious constraints upon what we might do in tailoring it to our personal advantage.

This line is persuasive so far as it goes. But it does not go far enough into the future to prove very compelling as an explanation of the fundamental phenomenon under consideration. For it is simply not credible that the reasons people have for wanting settled law into the foreseeable future necessarily commit them to having law settled beyond that point. The limiting case, perhaps, is that of someone like President Marcos, advocating one constitution so long as his re-election prospects under it looked rosy and another once his re-election prospects under the old one looked dim.

Few of us could reasonably expect to pull off that trick. Even President Marcos himself could not keep it up for long. But it entails no pragmatic contradiction for most of us to advocate one set of rules for the short to medium term, where the effects on our interests are tolerably predictable, while reserving our position for the longer term.[39] Agreeing to constitutional provisions on the understanding that they may be subject to renegotiation in twenty or thirty years is no more disruptive of

38 Elster (1988, pp. 8–14) argues this with specific reference to constitutions. Goodin (1990a) and Hardin (1988) deploy parallel arguments about instruments of political rule more generally in a rather different context, namely, the defence of utilitarianism against deontological critics.

39 An example of this style of provision (albeit one that was itself justified on profoundly different logic) might be Article I, Sect. 9 of the US Constitution, prohibiting Congress from outlawing the importation of slaves from abroad for the first twenty – but only the first twenty – years of the Constitution's operation.

our ordinary day-to-day affairs than is buying a fixed-term lease on a house that has only twenty or thirty years left to run. And keeping one's option for the further future open in that way is precisely the standard prescription for prudential agents in the face of substantial and ineluctable uncertainties.

Yet the point remains that, when faced with a "constitutional moment," most people do seem inclined to think – wholly or partly, gratuitously or otherwise – in the very long term. Certainly constitutional founders themselves are very conscious of acting under special circumstances and at a special moment.[40] It is crucial, they standardly say, for them to take advantage of that fact to make rules that will endure, in ways that ordinary laws might not.

Constitutions, unlike statutes, should, they say, aspire to "immortality." The American Founders proclaimed their desire that the US Constitution might "stand as fair a chance for immortality, as Lycurgus gave to that of Sparta, by making its change to depend on his own return" from beyond the grave.[41] And these sentiments were not purely for public consumption. Behind the closed doors of the Philadelphia drafting convention itself, James Madison had specifically appealed to delegates in these terms, "entreat[ing] the gentlemen representing the small states to renounce" their demand for equal representation for all states, large or small. This he described as a principle "which was confessedly unjust, which could never be admitted, and if admitted must infuse mortality into a Constitution which we wished to last forever."[42]

The puzzle here in view is why anyone sitting in Independence Hall listening to Madison should have deemed that a telling criticism. To put the point bluntly, why should anyone prefer institutions which work forever in an impartial way, to no one's advantage or disadvantage, when they could

40 Speaking in the Philadelphia Convention of 1787, Alexander Hamilton said, "We are weak and sensible of our weakness. Henceforward the motives will become feebler and the difficulites greater. It is a miracle that we are now here exercising our tranquil and free deliberations on the subject. It would be madness to trust to future miracles. A thousand causes must obstruct a reproduction of them" (Madison 1787, notes for 29 June, p. 216).

41 Madison, in Hamilton, Madison, and Jay 1788, no. 38, p. 246.

42 Madison 1787, notes for 29 June, p. 214.

have held out for ones which worked, with some certainty, to their own sectional advantage, at least for the foreseeable future?

There are many possible answers. It may well be, for example, that hold out as they may they could never realistically have gotten agreement on those more advantageous institutions anyway. But on the face of it, this hardly seems to be a strategy which would commend itself to prudence. Renouncing the pursuit of sectional interest – and, worse, doing so forever – hardly seems a proposition likely to appeal to delegates interested purely in sectional self-interest.

There are various other reasons, sectional interest apart, for constitutional founders valuing immortality in the institutions which they create. One such reason, and perhaps the most straightforward one, is that they wish thereby to secure immortality (or anyway the shadow of immortality) for themselves as the creators of those institutions.

But it is not purely a quest for personal immortality that is at work here. For constitutional framers would not be equally happy (or even at all happy) to perpetuate into the further future flawed or discreditable institutions. They seek right institutions, not just resilient ones. Stability for its own sake is clearly not their goal.[43]

Constitutions are cast in the relatively immutable form in which they characteristically are, then, at least in part out of high-minded moral principle. People want to think in the long term, when choosing the basic institutions of their society, even when they do not strictly need to do so. And they want to do that, at least in part, precisely because of the moral merits of projecting our collective reflections further into the future than any of us can selfishly calculate our own private advantage.

The same broad conclusions emerge from reflecting upon *how*, exactly, constitutions are made relatively immortal and immutable. Framers employ various devices in the attempt to make constitutions harder to alter than are ordinary statutes.

---

43 It is in part, perhaps, because founders want to be remembered for doing something good, not for perpetuating something bad. So the quest for personal immortality may still be playing a secondary role, here.

Constitutions typically embody rules for their amendment which are much more arduous than are required to enact or to alter ordinary legislation, involving everything from special assemblies to super-large majorities to repeated re-endorsement of proposed amendments by successive assemblies.[44]

Those provisions are typically branded as boring "housekeeping" aspects of constitutional law. They may be necessary for keeping the constitution in good order, all will readily concede. But they are not usually seen as central to the core constitutional enterprise. On my reading, they should be. The only thing that makes a constitution special – different from ordinary legislation – is that it is harder to alter. It is harder only because of the provision, within the constitution, specifying some especially arduous procedures for its own amendment.

Not only is it in some formalistic sense, then, in which the clause specifying procedures for amending a constitution is "the most fundamental" part of any constitutional text.[45] It is also the portion of the text which is the most fundamental in motivating moral behavior in the ways here in view. By ensuring that the constitution is hard to transform, such a clause makes us look further – and hence more impartially – into the distant future when discussing constitutional issues than when settling day-to-day political affairs.

The question, however, is why people bent on reforming the constitution regard such provisions as being particularly binding upon them. Some, no doubt, would regard it as "unthinkable for a[n American] constitutional Convention to propose the ratification of an amendment in a way that did not invoke the consent of three fourths of the states" – just as, for example, "it would be unthinkable . . . for a simple majority of [the

44 Friedrich 1968, chap. 8. Furthermore it is sometimes supposed that, in Cromwell's words, "there must be something Fundamental, something like a Magna Carta, which should be standing, should be unalterable" (quoted in Ibid., p. 136). Examples of constitutional provisions which are constitutionally beyond the power of anyone to alter are the French guarantee of a republican form of government (contained in an 1884 amendment) and the American guarantee that no state be deprived of equal representation in the Senate without its consent (Ibid., p. 145).

45 "Since it seeks to tell us the conditions under which all other constitutional texts and principles may be legitimately transformed" (Ackerman 1984, p. 1058).

American] Congress to enact a valid law over a presidential veto."[46]

But why should it be unthinkable? Recall that the Philadelphia Founders were themselves acting well beyond their formal brief, which directed them merely to propose amendments to the Articles of Confederation. The procedures they laid down for the adoption of the new Constitution, furthermore, did not correspond to stipulations of the old Articles. The Philadelphia Framers in effect staged a *coup d'état*. They did so, of course, in the name of, "We, the People." But why should not other subsequent, equally solemn convocations of Americans take it upon themselves to speak in similar terms?

The "formalist reading" of the Constitution "treats the Founders as an assemblage of demigods inhabiting a constitutional plane closed to subsequent generations." It "treats the Philadelphia Convention as if it existed on a different ontologial level from [subsequent] 'Conventions' convened by future generations of Americans."[47]

That practice is transparently indefensible, discredited in the very process of describing it. Surely, as Thomas Jefferson said in precisely this context, "Each generation is as independent of the one preceding, as that was of all which had gone before. It has . . ., like them, a right to choose for itself the form of government it believes most promotive of its own happiness. . . . [T]he dead have no rights."[48] Seen in that light, the Philadelphia Framers of the American Constitution, far from being demigods whose feats can never again be replicated by mere mortals, ought to "serve as the paradigmatic examples of a continuing constitutional possibility" open to all subsequent generations.[49]

Even if subsequent generations do not want to rewrite their constitution *tout court*, they might nonetheless consider the possibility of a partial rewriting of it, in ways that go outside the formal rules for amendment stipulated within the document itself. Again, American constitutional history offers a prime example: the Reconstruction Amendments, passed in the wake of the Union victory in the Civil War.

46   Ibid., p. 1060.
47   Ibid.
48   Sunstein 1988, p. 327.
49   Ackerman 1984, p. 1060.

When the Fourteenth Amendment was originally proposed by a Republican Congress in 1866, it was rejected by the state legislatures of ten formerly slave states and of three border states; that was more than enough vetoes to kill the Amendment, under the rules for amendment stipulated in Article V of the Constitution. Not prepared to take no for an answer, though, the Radical Republicans in Congress then passed the Reconstruction Acts instructing the Union Army of occupation to register freed blacks as voters in Southern state electorates.[50] Furthermore, "Section 5 of the first Reconstruction Act denied those new democratically elected state legislatures the authority to send senators and representatives to Congress on an equal footing with the other states until they ratified the Fourteenth Amendment!"[51]

This is pretty strong stuff. Against it all, Ackerman rightly inveighs:

> There is simply no way that this demand can be reconciled with the rules of Article V. If these rules mean anything, they deny Congress the authority to bootstrap its amendments to validity by destroying dissenting governments and then denying congressional representation to the new ones until they accept the constitutional initiatives that the preceding governments found unacceptable.[52]

The point of his invective ought not be mistaken, though. This is not offered as an argument against the Fourteenth Amendment, which Ackerman (and I) would wholeheartedly endorse. It is intended, instead, as an argument against a certain formalist view of what it takes to amend the Constitution.

Ackerman's point is not that the Fourteenth Amendment is invalid because adopted in ways contrary to Article V. He wants to claim, instead, that the Fourteenth Amendment is valid despite its having been adopted in ways contrary to the Constitution's self-prescribed procedures. It is one example (the New Deal is another) of an extraordinary "constitutional

---

50 Note that this was contrary to constitutional guarantees of a "republican form of government to each state," and prior to passage of the Fifteenth Amendment which retrospectively justifed such action.

51 Ackerman 1989a, p. 501.

52 Ibid., pp. 501–2.

moment" at which "We, the People" have taken a direct hand in the making and remaking of their constitution. The amendments thereby adopted are nonetheless valid for being adopted by some procedures outside the constitution. If anything, they are all the more valid for that fact.

Ackerman's concern, in telling this tale, is with the nature of constitutional law. I am less concerned with legal niceties. For present purposes, it hardly matters whether constitutional amendments that come about through extra-constitutional mechanisms ought or ought not to be considered "constitutional" – whether the old constitution has merely been amended, or whether it has been supplanted by another altogether (albeit one in most respects identical to the old). I merely want to note that, as a purely practical matter, it has proven possible for some bits of a constitution to be altered through extra-constitutional means without the rest of the constitutional fabric unraveling.

This raises, in turn, the question of why people who want to change the constitution consider themselves bound by the constitution's internal rules for its own amendment. Reflecting upon cases like this leads us to conclude that the "unthinkability" of altering constitutions by any but their own arduous, self-prescribed procedures is mostly a matter of individual self-restraint and collective self-delusion. It is mostly a myth, true only because and only insofar as we all collectively deem it to be so.[53] Any constraint thereby imposed is internal rather than external: it is not that it cannot be done, but rather that people self-censor the very thought that it might be done.

Again, there might be many reasons for such self-censorship. One reason – one explicitly given for reluctance to call another constitutional convention in the US – is the fear of opening Pandora's box. Everyone is naturally reluctant to risk reopening any part of the old constitutional settlement in a way that risks reopening all of it. Respecting the especially

---

53 The same is true of unwritten "norms" or "conventions of the constitution." What makes them special and especially impervious to change is the myth that they date from "time immemorial." But it is only the collective decision not to look too closely at the pretended histories that sustains this myth. For upon close inspection this "tradition" invariably dates just back to the day before yesterday and the historical lineage being claimed invariably proves to be only one among many equally valid interpretations of the past (Pocock 1957).

arduous internal mechanisms for amendment of the constitution guarantees that most things will stay settled while some few are being renegotiated.

That is a perfectly good, pragmatic reason for working through the constitution's internal amendment procedures. It nonetheless fails to explain why advocates of constitutional change, when they have the numbers politically required to ensure the precise outcomes that they want, tie their own hands by pursuing those goals in a constitutionally constrained fashion. Why not instead follow the lead of the Radical Republicans in railroading through the Reconstruction Amendments?

The reason, I suspect, is that people also have another more principled reason for working through the constitution's own internal amendment procedures. They want their constitution to last a long time – they want its basic provisions to be hard to change – precisely to avoid the special pleading that plagues ordinary legislative deliberations. The point of a "constitutional moment" is precisely that, in it, people should set aside their particular interests and internalize the "common good."[54] The point of a constitution is precisely that it should embody such shared understandings of the common good. And the point of respecting the especially arduous procedures prescribed within constitutions is precisely to ensure that outcome.

But then constitutions play a very different role than commonly imagined. Suppose people abide by the especially arduous procedures that constitutions prescribe for their own amendment only because of the greater impartiality of the ensuing outcomes. Then those constitutional provisions, far from making people behave more morally, once again merely reflect the fact that they are predisposed towards moral behavior in the first place. Constitutional provisions then do not play any important role in either ensuring or even evoking moral behavior. Rather, they merely register and reflect the fact that people were inclined that way all along.

There is an important element of "self-binding" at work in all this. Writing constitutions in ways so as to make them hard to change looks very much like the political equivalent of lashing oneself to a mast. Ordinarily people do so out of fear

54   Ackerman 1984; 1989. Wilson 1990.

of subsequent "weakness of will": they foresee that they will at some point be tempted to do what, both *ex ante* and *ex post*, they want not to do.[55]

What is involved in constitutionalism, thus construed, is not vacillation of the will, however. It is not as if people are, through constitutional provisions, trying to prevent momentary temptations from undermining their settled preferences. What they are trying to do through those mechanisms is to ensure the triumph of their own "higher" will over their "lower" one. It is not so much a matter of ensuring the triumph of the "interests" over the "passions" as it is of ensuring the triumph of people's impartial perception of the "common good" over their perception of their own particular interests. And insofar as constitutional constraints can bind us only so long as people are for the most part prepared to consider them binding, it must be the goal of agents themselves (and not just the aspirations of moral philosophers) that the "higher" triumph in this way over the lower.

If people are predisposed in this direction already, though, there is no reason to suppose that constitutionalism is the only mechanism that might give operational significance to those predispositions. A mechanism that makes people think far into the uncertain future is one way to make them – or, rather, to help them make themselves – adopt an impartial perspective upon the interests of all. But there are other mechanisms that serve equally well for people basically predisposed toward impartiality in the first place. A rule of "publicity" or "discursive defensibility" is another, which forms the focus of the next chapter.

55 Elster 1988; see more generally Davidson 1969 and Elster 1984. This is not an unprecedented way of thinking about constitutions, as Hume's (1739, bk 3, pt 2, sect. 7) argument, quoted above, makes clear.

SEVEN

Publicity, Accountability, and Discursive Defensibility

There is a parallelism in my discussion of political mechanisms for evoking moral behavior and my earlier discussion of moral mechanisms. In both cases, I have proceeded from mechanisms making less direct appeals to people's internalized moral motives to mechanisms making more direct appeals to them. It has turned out that even mechanisms making minimal direct appeals to morality as such may nonetheless require some such appeal at some central point early in the argument. That has proven as true of the role of constitutionalism, politically, as it did of the role of uncertainty, morally.

The final political mechanism here in view – the "rule of publicity" – would appear to rest more directly still upon an appeal to people's internalized moral principles. In its most fundamental form, publicity will work to make people behave more morally only insofar as they would be embarrassed at being seen to behave indefensibly or immorally; and for that sanction to have any bite, people must obviously internalize if not morality itself then at least others' moral opinions of them.

Philosophically, the most classic formulation of the "rule of publicity" is probably Kant's: "all actions affecting the rights of other human beings are wrong if their maxim is not compatible with their being made public."[1] Various contemporary

1 Kant 1795, p. 126. Bentham reaches much the same conclusions by a rather different route in his discussion of the "public character of law" (Postema 1989).

philosophers – among them, Rawls, Ackerman, and most especially Habermas – have spilled considerable ink trying to work out exactly what it means to govern your life only by principles that you are able to defend in dialogue with other people.[2] Those theories will be discussed shortly. But as for initial illustrations of this strategy, perhaps it would be better to stick to some more frankly political examples rather than retreating immediately to anything so abstract as Kant's "transcendental formula of public good" and its equally obscure progeny.

The general idea at work, here, is politically perfectly familiar. William Godwin put it well, in his tract on *Political Justice*: "Virtue will always be an unusual spectacle among men, till they shall have learned to be at all times ready to avow their actions, and assign the reasons upon which they are founded."[3] Or, in the pithier phrases of the Reverend Sydney Smith, "It is not enough that a political institution works well practically: it must be defensible; it must be such as will bear discussion, and not excite ridicule and contempt."

The unreformed British Parliament – characterized as it was by "rotten boroughs" (i.e., constituencies with only a handful of electors) and the buying and selling of political influence – invited precisely that, as Smith proceeded to show. "It might work well for all I know," says the Reverend Smith, "if, like the savages of Onelashka, we send out to catch a king: but who could defend a coronation by chase? who," by the same token, "can defend the payment of £40,000 for the three-hundredth part of the power of Parliament, and the resale of this power to Government for places" in the Lords?[4] The general idea that the obligation to explain and defend ourselves

2   Rawls 1971, p. 133; 1985; 1987. Ackerman 1980; 1989b. Habermas 1973, discussed in Pettit 1982 and Elster 1986. In his stinging critique of this whole program, Walzer (1989/90, p. 184) protests that the quest for "truth" or "moral rightness" through a conversation presupposes a "hypothetical" rather than an actual conversation, governed according to "a design, a set of rules, which will determine who exactly the protagonists are and what they can say. . . . Curiously, once one has a conversational design" of that sort, "it is hardly necessary to have a conversation" at all. In other words, we see here another case of "morality in, morality out." The conversational device is doing no work for us.
3   Godwin 1798, bk 6, chap. 10.
4   Smith 1831, p. 346.

in public discussion somehow makes us behave more morally is, then, not a particularly rare or novel thought.

Here, though, let us consider three more extended examples of particular sorts of political institutions and practices that, by forcing this obligation upon us, might make us behave more morally than we otherwise would have done in our political affairs. Consider first President Woodrow Wilson's doctrine of "open covenants openly arrived at." That, perhaps, is the very best example of a person in high political office self-consciously evoking the morally cleansing powers of "publicity" and of requirements of "discursive defensibility." Wilson was no latter-day convert. The attack on secret diplomacy and corrupt closed-door practices had been a centerpiece of the Progressive movement from which Wilson sprang. The publisher Joseph Pulitzer was merely echoing – however self-servingly – the widespread popular view of the age when saying, "publicity, publicity, publicity, is the greatest moral factor and force in our public life." And Wilson himself had campaigned for the White House claiming that "publicity is one of the purifying elements of politics. Nothing checks all the bad practices of politics like public exposure."[5]

Against this background, it is hardly surprising that Wilson made "open covenants openly arrived at" the very first among his Fourteen Points defining the American position in the Treaty of Versailles negotiations. And, perhaps equally important-antly in the context of the present argument, he prefaced that demand with some conspicuously Golden Rule style rhetoric. Let me quote the *obiter* as well as the *dictum*, then, to give the full flavor of the Wilsonian doctrine. "What we demand in this war," the President said in expounding the country's war aims before Congress,

> is nothing peculiar to ourselves. It is that the world are in effect partners in this interest, and for our own part we see very clearly that unless justice be done to others it will not be done to us. The program of the world's peace, therefore, is our program; and that program, the only possible program, as we see it, is this.

5 Safire 1978, p. 536. The theme was not unique to the Progressives, though. Ralph Waldo Emerson, long before them, had written in his essay on "The Conduct of Life" that, "As gaslight is found to be the best nocturnal police, so the universe protects itself by pitiless publicity."

Then Wilson proceeded to set out his Fourteen Points, the first of which insisted upon:

> Open covenants of peace, openly arrived at, after which there shall be no private international understandings of any kind, but diplomacy shall proceed always frankly and in the public view.[6]

Of course, that was easier said in Washington than done in Paris, and all too soon Wilson found himself forced to backpeddle, at least on that second clause. Even before negotiations got underway, Wilson had to send the inestimable Colonel House around to explain to Clemenceau and Lloyd George that of course the President's "intention was not to exclude confidential diplomatic negotiations involving delicate matters"; the President meant merely "to insist that nothing which occurs in the course of such confidential negotiations shall be binding unless it appears in the final covenant made public to the world."[7] So much for the bit about "openly arrived at."

Still, for better or worse, Wilson made the "open covenants' bit of his demand stick.[8] And that at least arguably was enough for purposes of fixing leaders in the glare of publicity, and requiring them to explain and defend to their followers what they had done.

Another example of an institution that had similar effects, in terms of forcing people to explain and to defend their actions publicly, is "open voting" – the practice of literally calling out your vote for all to hear, or of inserting into the ballot box a colour-coded party list for all to see. The example seems so quaint today that it is hard to recall how very standard the practice was in its day, and how very late into the last century it persisted.

The reasons for ending open voting and instituting the secret ballot instead are easy enough to recall: eliminating the undue influence exerted by landlords over tenants, customers over shop-keepers, trade-unionists over their fellow workers, and

6 Wilson 1918.
7 Safire 1978, p. 492.
8 "For better or worse" because the troubles he had in making it stick might have contributed to Wilson's inability to muster sufficient support in America for ratification of the treaty (Bailey 1944).

such like.[9] The arguments against the secret ballot, and in favor of open voting, are less easily recalled. In the present context, however, they are the more important.[10]

Typical objections to the secret ballot in the nineteenth century were cast in terms of cowardice.[11] Rev Sydney Smith, for example, complains that the secret ballot "compels those persons . . . who glory in the cause they support . . . to conceal their votes." He mockingly advises advocates of secret votes, "If you are afraid to go in at the front door and to say in a clear voice what you have to say, go in at the back door and say it in a whisper – but . . . you make me, who am bold and honest, sneak in at the back door as well as yourself." Similar sentiments recur in the more succinct words of a mid-century US senator, "I want to see every man an independent voter, not sneaking to the polls and hiding his expression in a secret ballot."[12]

Far more important than that simple issue of cowardice, however, is the danger that different – and more debased – opinions would be expressed in private than in public. The hope of the reformers was, of course, precisely the opposite: they wanted to free voters from the effects of bribery and intimidation, in order that they could vote their true opinions in uncorrupted fashion. But opponents of the secret ballot feared that it would bring with it corruption of another and potentially far worse sort. The arguments of John Stuart Mill against the secret ballot are particularly worth recalling:

> A great number of the electors will have two sets of preferences – those on private, and those on public

9   The latter weighed most heavily with the elites responsible for instituting the secret ballot; see Bendix and Rokkan 1964, p. 100. Cf. Smith 1839; Mill 1861, chap. 10; and Brennan and Pettit 1990.

10   They are being resurrected, though, by Brennan and Pettit 1990.

11   In earlier periods, writers could say more forthrightly that "the lower class ought to be directed by those of higher rank and restrained . . . by the gravity of eminent personages" which "was no longer possible" once voting was done in secret (Montesquieu 1748, bk 2, sect. 2).

12   Senator Lyman Trumbull, quoted in Brennan and Pettit 1990. Smith 1839, p. 351. See similarly Godwin 1798, bk 6, chap. 10. Bendix and Rokkan (1964, p. 100) comment that "the Prussian system of oral voting was [also] defended in these terms, but was maintained for so long largely becaue it proved an easy way of controlling the votes of farm laborers."

grounds. The last are the only ones which the elector would like to avow. The best side of their character is that which people are anxious to show, even to those who are no better than themselves. People will give dishonest or mean votes from lucre, from malice, from pique, from personal rivalry, even from the interests or prejudices of class or sect, more readily in secret than in public.[13]

For Mill and his fellow opponents of the secret ballot, then, voting openly and publicly was justified as a means of forcing people to act from higher, more noble motives – from motives that they could espouse and defend in public discourse, under challenge from their fellow citizens.[14]

In this, Mill's speculation seems to be borne out by at least one fascinating bit of anthropological evidence. The study in question mapped the evolution of decisions over time in a Thai village. Its particularly striking finding, in line with Mill's conjecture, is that in the course of protracted public discussions more equitable and more public-spirited motives seem to come to the fore. More selfish and particularistic motives, in contrast, seem to recede over the course of those discussions.[15]

Finally, consider the experience of the Office of Emergency Preparedness Administration, the agency responsible for administering President Nixon's wage-price freeze. As might be expected, people were forever petitioning, disingenuously or otherwise, to have their own cases treated as exceptions to the general rules. As might also be expected, the OEPA developed a good line by way of relatively automatic, knee-jerk replies to such petitions.

The consequence is that anyone who merely wrote in with a request for a variation in the ordinary rules got short shrift. It was rough justice, usually – but not invariably – richly

13 Mill 1861, p. 311; see further Brennan and Pettit 1990.
14 The argument can work both ways, of course. It might equally well be said, as Bendix and Rokkan (1964, p. 100) do, that "the provisions for secrecy isolate the dependent worker not only from his superiors but also from his peers. . . . The provision for secret voting thus puts the individual before a personal choice and makes him at least temporarily independent of his immediate enviornment: in the voting booth he can be a national citizen."
15 Bilmes 1979, pp. 175–6.

deserved. Just occasionally, however, such summary justice failed actually to do justice in a genuinely anomalous case. There is where a personal visit to the OEPA office came in. And there is where, for the present purposes, the story really begins.

Students of administrative behavior, examining the effects of these personal appeals, note a marked difference in the disposition of cases presented by post and in person. The difference is such as to suggest that administrators manifest a markedly more moral attitude in those cases in which they have to explain and defend their decisions in person – to someone sitting just across a desk from them, rather than to someone reading their bureaucratese thousands of miles away. "Whenever an inquirer arranged to present his case in person, he almost automatically broke through any propensity toward blatantly legalistic or retreatist case processing. The agency official who met the inquirer face-to-face . . . was forced to attend to the fairness and economic impact of the decision."[16] And this was reflected in the markedly different outcomes of official deliberations in the two kinds of cases: "while two-thirds of the relatively few cases (ten percent) presented in person received accommodative answers, only one-third of the many inquiries presented in writing had their prayers answered."[17]

Open voting is definitely dead, and open diplomacy may well be dead or dying. But let us step back from those particular practices to see what more general philosophical lessons they might hold for us. There are, after all, a great many really rather different reasons that we might have in endorsing the general Kantian demand for a rule of "publicity" or, in its contemporary terms, of "discursive defensibility" to govern public life.[18]

Some of those reasons are purely pragmatic. If we take a realist view of moral truth as being truth like any other, then (by a simple extension of Rousseau or Mill or the consensus theory of truth) we can easily enough see the advantage of a

16   Kagan 1978, p. 152.
17   Ibid.; Kagan goes on to add, "Nor are these differences explained by any other likely factors."
18   See, more generally, Habermas 1964/1974 and Dryzek 1990.

free and open discussion of moral norms and public policies predicated upon them.[19] Equally pragmatically, we can say that, at the very least, laws must be public – promulgated and publicized – if they are to serve as laws at all. Secret laws simply cannot be self-consciously followed.[20] And it will be easier to learn and to recall those rules if the reasons underlying them are publicly available as well.[21] Beyond all those pragmatic reasons for publicity, there are other, more principled ones. Advocates of autonomy, after the fashion of Rousseau and Kant, would regard it as particularly important that reasons for rules be accessible to agents, in order that they can indeed make those rules their own and act only from commands that they have given to themselves.[22]

I mention all those considerations – pragmatic as well as principled – merely to set them to one side for present purposes. They may well all be valid arguments. On that I pass no judgment. They are just not what I am interested in here.

Recall the context in which our discussion of publicity has arisen. The question is how to arrange our political affairs so as to motivate people to behave morally. And for purposes of this argument, I do not want to presuppose any particular theory of morality (e.g., Rousseau or Kant's autonomy-based

19 Rousseau 1762, bk 4, chap 2. Mill 1859, chap. 2. Habermas (1973, pp. 102–11) seems to be arguing essentially this line; see Pettit 1982. It is pretty clearly what is suggested in Vanberg and Buchanan's (1989) interpretation and application of Habermas' theory; they assign "dialogue" the role of assessing the "theory component" of constitutional choice, and propose in that connection a standard by which "agreement" represents a "truth judgment" rather than merely a compromise between competing interests.

20 Fuller 1969, pp. 49–51. Of course, people might always follow a rule without knowing it. And, under American Constitutional law at least, Presidential proclamations take legal effect from the moment they are signed and sealed in the proper form whether or not they have yet been published (Tulis 1987, p. 54). The point is not that unpublished laws are conceptually incapable of being laws at all, somehow. The point is just that they are incapable of doing what laws are ordinarily supposed to do – i.e., guide people's behavior – if they are not promulgated.

21 Rawls 1971, p. 133.

22 Rousseau 1762, bk 1, chap. 6. Kant 1785. Rawls's more recent work, focusing upon the "accessibility" of particular styles of reasons to particular sorts of agents in societies like our own, seems to work more in this vein; see Rawls 1985; 1987.

ethic). Instead, I want to work simply with the most noncontentious sort of Golden Rule ethical standards available.

In previous chapters, the requirements of that sort of ethic were clear enough. There, it was the politics or sociology of the matter – how to motivate people to act upon those principles – that required elucidation. Here, the political device is clear. The proposal is that we use publicity, in one form or another, to evoke moral behavior. Here, it is the ethics of the matter that require elaboration. In what sense might the actions that people take, knowing that they will have to defend those actions in public, be more moral – in this most noncontentious sense of being more in compliance with the Golden Rule?

At root, the way a rule of publicity and discursive defensibility works to ensure Golden Rule style outcomes must be something like this: "There are certain arguments that simply cannot be stated publicly. In a political debate it is pragmatically impossible to argue that a given solution should be chosen just because it is good for oneself. By the very act of engaging in a public debate – by arguing rather than bargaining – one has ruled out the possibility of invoking such reasons."[23] The general idea, in other words, seems to be that the necessity of defending your position in public discussion rules out any form of special pleading. You cannot expect others to cut you special deals that you are not prepared to cut for them. And universalization of that form – enforced, here, by the simple need to defend yourself in public discussion – is what the Golden Rule ethic is all about.

We must be careful not to claim too much for this model. Habermas, for example, seems to think that the exigencies of unconstrained conversations will somehow force us to attend to the "common good" rather than to "special interests" not shared with others.[24] In this, he is quite plainly wrong. All that having to defend yourself in unconstrained public discussion implies is that you cannot expect others to buy an argument

23 Elster 1986, pp. 112–13. He credits this thought, in turn, to Midgaard (1980); see further Midgaard, Stenstadvold, and Underdal 1973. Habermas (1973, pp. 111–17) argues similarly; see further Pettit 1982, pp. 225–6.
24 Habermas (1973, p. 108), for example, writes that, "The interest is common because the constraint-free consensus permits only what all can want." See, more generally, Habermas 1973, pt 3 and Pettit 1982, pp. 225–6.

from you that you would not be willing to buy from them. But that is perfectly consistent with log-rolling of the ordinary sort: I will support you in pursuit of your narrow self-interest if you support me in pursuit of mine.

Thus, it should come as no particular surprise that "the trading of votes" is "occasionally . . . done quite openly in the course of public debate." As an example of this, recall an exchange that took place on the floor of the US Senate during a 1956 debate on agricultural subsidies:

Mr Langer (North Dakota):	We don't raise any tobacco in North Dakota, but we are interested in the tobacco situation in Kentucky, and I hope the Senator [from that state] will support us in securing assistance for wheat growers in our state.
Mr Clements (Kentucky):	I think the Senator will find that my support will be 100 percent.
Mr Barkely (Kentucky):	Mr President, will my colleague from Kentucky yield [the floor]?
Mr Clements:	I yield.
Mr Barkley:	The colloquy just [heard] confirms and justifies the Woodrow Wilsonian doctrine of open covenants openly arrived at. *(Laughter).*[25]

The fact that the senators laughed at Senator Barkley's joke suggests, of course, that they thought it slightly inappropriate that deals should be struck quite so openly and blatantly on the floor of the Senate. But notice that the presiding officer made no move to rule the colloquy out of order either. There is nothing inherent in the logic of public discourse that guarantees that the "general will," rather than the mere "will of all" (the mere aggregate of people's selfish interests), will emerge from those discussions.[26]

25 Quoted in *Mathews 1960, pp. 99–100*.
26 The terms are, of course, Rousseau's (1762). Notice, however, that his ideal mode of evoking the general will was one that averted the need for any discussion whatsoever; see Rousseau 1762, bk 2, chap. 3 and bk 4, chaps 1 and 2.

In taking care not to claim too much for the model, however, we must take care not to claim too little for it either. What having to defend ourselves in the course of free and open public discussions will do is force us to appeal to justifications that are universal in form. True, universal egoism – the rule that each should look out for his or her own interests – is as universalizable a rule as any other. But forcing us to universalize our egoism in this way, and to accept that it is as legitimate for others to try to steal from us as it is for us to try to steal from them, is no mean feat. Universalizing our egoism is a crucial first step, albeit in itself perhaps a pathetically small one, down the path toward a Golden Rule ethic.

A t this point, though, it pays to explore a little more deeply exactly how it might happen that simply having to explain and defend yourself in public discourse might force you to internalize norms of a Golden Rule sort. There are, in fact, two quite distinct ways in which this might work.

The first model – more familiar, and perhaps less interesting for that reason – explains the connection in a straightforwardly political manner. On this model, the reason you impose constraints of universalizability on the arguments you employ in public discussions is that you are looking for argumentative allies. This makes most sense, of course, when the argument is taking place in an explicitly vote-counting forum, like the US Senate. But it might make a fair bit of sense even in contexts where the weight of numbers makes itself felt more subtly and informally.

Insofar as the name of the game is to win allies and votes, it is transparently clear why you should want to cast your arguments in terms that will appeal to others. But there, it is not the simple logic of public discourse that has somehow forced you to internalize Golden-Rule style norms. It is, instead, the political exigencies of vote-counting that has done the trick.[27]

The second model, therefore, is the rather more interesting

---

27   That is precisely how norms of "accountability" have classically worked, of course. See Johnson 1974, Stanyer 1974 and Day and Klein 1987. But that is explicitly *not* the way writers like Habermas (1973, pp. 111–17) would want to make the connection: Habermas scorns this as a model of mere "compromise," to be sharply distinguished from his preferred model of rational discursive consensus.

one. Here, the claim is that having to explain and defend yourself in public genuinely does make you *internalize*, in a properly psychological sense, Golden-Rule norms. What motivates you, on this model, is not the fear of losing support of others but rather sheer embarrassment at the utter inappropriateness of certain styles of arguments in the public forum.

That is not to say that external pressure is completely unnecessary on this model. It may well have been necessary to bring external pressure to bear to get you into the public forum in the first place. English monarchs traditionally operated under the rule, "Kings render no accounts"; and it took the Glorious Revolution of 1688 to persuade them otherwise.[28] But once external pressure of that sort has managed to bring people to the public forum and oblige them to give an account of themselves, it may well be that the pressure then to appeal only to arguments that are universal in form is wholly internalized, emanating from within rather than without.[29]

The implications of this argument, if true, would be highly important. Those of us schooled in broadly Hobbesian traditions of *realpolitik* might suppose that mechanisms of accountability matter only if – and only so far as – some serious sanction can and will be levelled, if the account that is offered proves unacceptable. And the infrequency (indeed, frequently the total absence) of any serious sanctioning – bad publicity and public embarrassment apart – makes us very suspicious of what we would therefore regard as "toothless" accountability mechanisms.

But we have now seen that accountability mechanisms may work in some other way instead. They may work by forcing people to internalize Golden Rule norms, in anticipation of a public accounting. If people will be suitably embarrassed and ashamed at having to admit in public that their conduct cannot be defended in those terms, then perhaps they can be persuaded to reshape their conduct in such a way as to avoid later having to make any such embarrassing admissions.

This is no merely theoretical possibility: arguably, at least, these effects are very real. Consider the case of corporate crime. Many argue that publicity of corporate misconduct is at

28 Day and Klein 1987, pp. 13–14.
29 Scott and Lyman 1968.

least as effective sanction as any fines that might be imposed.[30] Or, for a more frankly political example, consider a recent study of the impact of US legislation requiring all government agencies to file an Environmental Impact Statement before undertaking any major new public works. Skeptics said that merely filing a statement was a toothless mechanism for restraining agencies otherwise disposed to wreck havoc on the environment. But it turns out not to be so. Just forcing people to fill in the blanks under certain headings, and to make a public declaration of their answers, seems to have been enough to secure substantial shifts in behavior. The evidence suggests that US government agencies are much more sensitive to environmental considerations – both much more conscious of and much more solicitous toward those interests – simply by reason of having to make that public declaration.[31]

Realpolitik skeptics may well remain unconvinced. The constraint of having to give a public account need not be all that constraining, for people who really do not want it to be. Rhetorical tricks are cheap and easy and, at least in the short term, reasonably successful.[32] Any given action admits of multiple interpretations; it should not be all that hard to find some interpretation or another that will appeal to others, even if it was not your real motive for acting.[33]

The advocate of the public-discourse strategy for evoking Golden Rule behavior has two options, at this point. One is to go the whole hog for a psychological story. Forcing you to explain and defend yourself in free and open public discussions forces you at least to *talk* in Golden Rule terms; and if you talk that way long enough, you will inevitably start *thinking* that way, too. So, while you might start out dissimilating, pretending noble motives that were not really your own, in the end you will come around to making them your own. Or so the thoroughly psychological story would have it.[34]

30   Fisse and Braithwaite 1983.
31   Taylor 1984.
32   Goodin 1980, chap. 4.
33   Goodin 1989. Elster 1986, pp. 118–19.
34   Elster 1986, p. 113. For those, such as Habermas (1973) and Dryzek (1990, chaps 2 and 3), who want to claim that the outcomes of such unconstrained conversations are uniquely rational, the intervention of irrational psychological mechanisms such as dissonance-reduction would be damaging; Elster (1986, p. 113) is perfectly right about that.

There is no need to evoke anything quite so dramatic as that, though. We can simply build upon the presumption that people have a certain latent "moral sense" within them. Motivating moral behavior at all presupposes something like that, anyway: if we are to get a motivational grip on people, there must already be something within them for us to grip onto. The function of public accountability requirements might simply be to appeal to people's moral sense and to remind them of its requirements. And encouraging people to ask themselves "How would this sound in a public statement?" might just be one way of giving substance to the diffuse Golden Rule norms that they internalize already.[35] It is not that they could not lie about their true motives: the *realpolitik* skeptic is perfectly right to say that they could. It is just that they would not really want to.

Realpolitik analysts might still be unsatisfied. Their objection was that the obligation merely to "tell a good story" in a public

---

My claim is merely that the outcomes are more moral, not necessarily more rational. Consider as an example of that the social psychological experiments involving the role of discussion among groups facing Prisoner Dilemma situations: people who have discussed the matter with one another and promised to behave cooperatively are significantly more likely to behave cooperatively, even though in the peculiar context of that game it remains singularly irrational to do so (Dawes, McTavish, and Shaklee 1977; Orbell, von de Kragt and Dawes 1988).

35 That, Myrdal (1944, pp. 1028–9) says, is how "government by discussion" works. "The individual . . . does not act in moral isolation. He is not left alone to manage his rationalizations as he pleases without interference from outside. His valuations will, instead, be questioned and disputed. . . . It is not that the one claims to have certain valuations that the other does not have. It is rather an appeal to valuations which the other keeps in the shadow of inattention, but which are assumed, nonetheless, to be actually held in common. This assumption . . . is ordinarily correct!. . . . In this process of moral criticism which men make upon each other, the valuations on the higher and more general planes – referring to *all* human beings and *not* to specific small groups – are regularly invoked by one party or the other, simply because they are held in common among all groups in society, and also because of the supreme prestige they are traditionally awarded. By this democratic process of open discussion more is made concious than any single person or group would on his own initiative find it advantageous to bring forward at the particular moment. . . . This effect . . . is the principal reason why we . . . hold that public discussion is purifying and that democracy itself provides a moral education of the people."

forum imposed constraints that were too weak. People who really wanted to behave badly still could. All that I have said, in the end, is that it will prove a pretty useful reminder for someone who already wants to behave well, and it will serve as useful training for those who are capable of being persuaded to behave better. In short, I confess that I cannot crack the really tough nut, the person who really wants to behave badly. My suggestion is simply that we not waste quite so much time trying. To do so simply misallocates our moral energies, as was argued at the outset.

We nonetheless ought to have genuine reservations about the model of publicity, accountability, and discursive defensibility as a mechanism for evoking moral behavior. They are of a very different kind than the *realpolitik* skeptic's, but they are no less deep.

The model of discursive defensibility presupposes free and open discussions. People must be allowed to say anything they want, to challenge anything they want. Everyone must be on an equal conversational footing. No person, and no position, should be able to make a preemptory claim of privilege by reason of "authority" or whatever. No person, and no position, should be ruled out of court, right from the start. Those conditions are required, not just to make the conversation a rational one, but also to make its conclusions morally meritorious.[36] It is only if every person and every positions is, conversationally, on an equal footing that the conversation can hope fully to implement the precepts of Golden Rule universality.

Yet the point remains that there are some views that we want to keep off the conversational agenda. There are certain views – racist or sexist or nativist views, for example – that we think it better not to have expressed in the public forum. The reason is not that there is any danger that they might prevail. The reason is, rather, that they will give unnecessary offense, even if ultimately they lose out in the voting.[37] As Shklar says, "We expect to behave better as citizens and public officials than as actors in the private sphere. . . . It is, for example, no

36   The conditions, of course, are just those of Habermas" "ideal speech situation": see Pettit 1982, Elster 1986 and Midgaard 1980.
37   Goodin 1986, pp. 91–6.

longer acceptable to make racist or anti-Semitic remarks in public in America; yet in private conversation racism and anti-Semitism are expressed as freely and as frequently as ever." She goes on to ask, rhetorically, "Would [anyone] prefer more public frankness? Should our public conduct really mirror our private, inner selves?"[38] The answer, presumably, is no.

It is at least partly in appreciation of such points that legislatures have, from time to time, imposed upon themselves various sorts of "gag rules."[39] Some of the things you are not allowed to say on the floor of the legislative chamber are matters of little consequence – matters of mere decorum rather than of political substance. Nothing in the substance of the political debate is changed by the requirement that legislators refrain from addressing each other by name, for example. But some of the restrictions on what can be said are of more political consequence. The British prohibition on Members of Parliament employing "treasonable or seditious language or a disrespectful use of Her Majesty's name" did indeed touch upon a substantively contentious issue, so far as Irish nationalist MPs were concerned; and they kept getting thrown out of the chamber for violating it, in the early years of this century.[40] Much the same is true of the self-denying ordinance, in force in the US House of Representatives from 1836 to 1845, simply not to debate any motion arising on the subject of slavery.[41]

38 Shklar 1979, p. 19.
39 Holmes 1988. Ackerman makes a superficially similar proposal for "conversational restraint," where basic premises cannot be agreed; but note well that is "principle of conversational restraint does not apply to the questions citizens may ask, but [merely] to the answers they may legitimately give to each other's questions" (Ackerman 1989b, p. 17). The "gag rules" here under discussion, of course, serve precisely to keep certain questions off the agenda altogether, rather than merely serving to constrain what might be said for and against various proposals once they are on the agenda.
40 May 1971, p. 415. Taylor 1971, pp. 98–9.
41 Holmes 1988, pp. 31–5. Lest that be thought some peculiarity of parliamentary maneuvering, consider Abraham Lincoln's similar remarks *en route* to his Inauguration: "In every crowd through which I have passed of late some allusion has been made to the present distracted condition of the country [i.e., the threatened secession of the Southern states]. It is naturally expected that I should say something upon this subject, but to touch upon it at all would involve an elaborate discussion of a great many questions and circumstances, would require more time than I can at present command, and would, perhaps, unnecessarily commit me

The point about all these gag rules is not just that they specify things that should not be done. More to the point, they specify things that should not even be discussed, in official public fora at least. And the reason they should not be discussed is not just that they should not be done. (If that were the only fear, then we could trust to the ordinary workings of free and open discussion – governed as it inevitably is by Golden-Rule logic – to kill off immoral proposals once they are put to the vote.) The wrongness of discussing such proposals is somehow independent of the wrongness of carrying them out.

These examples of legislative gag rules may or may not be particularly meritorious in their own right. (The prohibition on abolitionist petitions in the US Congress strikes me as most unfortunate, in all sorts of ways, for example.) The general issue, though, seems to be an important one. There are simply some things that are better left unsaid. That being so, the model of discursive defensibility – presupposing as it does wholly unconstrained conversations – is open to serious question.

L et us close, then, by examining in a little more detail two examples of cases in which the morally superior outcome was arguably better served by leaving certain things unsaid. As always, these cases are not completely clearcut. In the first of them, which side truly holds the high moral ground is perhaps disputable (certainly it has been politically disputed, anyway). In the second, the morality of the matter is clearer but the sociology of the matter less so. But since each of these examples displays symmetrical defects, perhaps the strengths of the one can compensate for the weaknesses of the other. The pair, taken together, might in that way prove more than either example alone could hope to establish.

The first example to be discussed concerns the politics of abortion in the United States. Let us simply take it as given, for purposes of this example: (a) that the moral truth lies with those who think that a woman should legally have the right to

---

upon matters which have not yet fully developed themselves." The reporter records, at that point, "Immense cheering and cries of good! [and] that's right!" (Lincoln's speech of 15 February 1861 in Pittsburgh, Pa, quoted in Tulis 1987, p. 5).

choose what happens to her own body; and (b) that that implies a right to abort an unwanted fetus, at least right up to the point at which that fetus is capable of sustaining an independent existence outside the mother's body. That proposition can, at the very least, aspire to the status of a "generational truth": "people who have come of sexual age . . . [during the last two decades simply] take it for granted that fertility decisions are to be made only by the individuals involved."[42]

That proposition is still contentious in many other circles, of course, and those opposing abortion obviously do so out of high moral principle: that is the sense in which this first example is messy because the morality of the matter is contestable. But since the interest of the example is primarily sociological anyway, let us try to take the morality of allowing abortions in the first trimester of pregnancy as given and see how the political sociology of the situation unfolds.

The part of the story deserving particular attention in the present context is just this. Advocates of women's rights were winning the fight here until they were foolish enough to declare war. The story, on Kristen Luker's able telling of the tale, seems to go roughly as follows. Physicians had always been allowed to perform abortions legally, so long as they could defend them as "therapeutic" to a committee of their peers. So long as the "abortion was performed by a 'reputable' physician in good standing in the community, who consulted with colleagues about the indications for the abortion, and performed it in an 'above-board' fashion from motives that were seen as 'humanitarian' rather than commercial, that abortion was very likely to be defined as therapeutic" and hence legal.[43] Then, "in 1959, the American Law Institute . . . drafted a model statute that" would, in effect, have "provided legal permission for performing the sorts of abortions that . . . physicians [had been] performing anyway."[44] When a

---

42 Luker 1984, p. 242. They suppose that there should be some such *legal* right, whether or not they also think that women should be absolutely at liberty, morally, to exercise that right just as they please.
43 Ibid., p. 73.
44 Ibid., pp. 69–70. Specifically, the Model Law would have "approved abortion in cases where it was necessary to protect the life and health of the mother (including her mental health) in cases of rape and incest, and in cases where there was a probability of congenital defects appearing in the embryo."

freshman state legislator in California set about introducing it into the Assembly, his mentor, a member of the powerful Rules Committee, asked him, "Have you ever met Cardinal MacIntyre?" "No" replied the young legislator. "You're about to" said his mentor, uttering words that can hardly have been more prophetic.[45]

Public discussion of that bill came to focus upon one case in particular, that of a woman seeking to abort a fetus likely deformed by the Thalidomide that she had taken in early pregnancy. Mobilization and counter-mobilization of the most politically charged sort ensued, and the process was spurred on by the Supreme Court's taking it upon itself, in *Roe v. Wade*, to impose as a constitutional edict what the American Law Institute had commended merely for legislative discussion. The upshot was a singularly unhappy one: the prohibition of federal funding for the abortions of government employees, members of the military and their dependents; a Republican Party platform that supports a constitutional amendment banning abortion; and various fire-bombings of abortion clinics.[46]

The lesson to be learned from this case, it would seem, is indeed a lesson about how it is morally better to leave certain things unstated. On Luker's reading, the lesson of the story is this:

> Prior to the reform movements of the 1960s, the presence of a strict law [against abortion] satisfied those who wanted to believe that virtually all abortions should be outlawed, whereas the much broader interpretation of the law in actual medical practice satisfied those who felt that embryos were only potential persons and that embryonic rights were far less compelling than the rights of mothers. Since the fundamental ideological differences between the two views were hidden from the public (to be weighted in individual cases by individual doctors), this form of compromise worked reasonably well for many years.[47]

45   Ibid., pp. 73, 69–70.
46   Ibid., p. 216.
47   Ibid., p. 77. Whether that compromise was a stable one in the long term is an open question. It may well be the case that the illusion that abortions were carried out only in special circumstances could not have been sustained for much longer, anyway, in the face of mounting demands for them from a new, "liberated" generation of women.

In short, the advocates of women's rights were winning the battle until they declared the war.

For our second extended example, let us consider a case where the morals of the matter are more clearcut. Presumably no one can seriously deny that morality, in its starkest Golden Rule form, requires that no one be educationally disadvantaged by public institutions on account of race alone.[48] That just means that state schools should provide educational opportunities that are equal for all. Minimally, that means in turn that, for example, blacks not be forced to suffer the sort of overcrowding and lack of basic instructional materials which are all too often found nowadays in black inner-city schools in America but which are absent in white suburban schools. Beyond that, though, it would also mean that those with special educational needs be specially catered for. Again, let us simply take that moral standard as given, and explore the sociology of the matter.

Here again, the theme is one of how we can achieve morally superior outcomes by leaving certain things unsaid. Specifically, consider David Kirp's excellent discussion of the virtues of the British policy of "inexplicitness' in dealing with issues of race and schooling. In his book *Doing Good By Doing Little*, Kirp writes,

> With as little fuss as possible, Britain has gone about the business of providing an education for its ever-growing number of nonwhite children. . . . At present, there exist no educational programs aimed directly at nonwhites, no deliberate efforts to school nonwhites and whites together, and little concern with the possibility of racial discrimination in education. At least as a matter of official educational policy, the British minimize the relevance of color.[49]

48 To say no one can deny that proposition is not, of course, to say that no one has or will done so: modal operators operate very curiously indeed in politics.

49 Kirp 1979, pp. 1–2. The quotation continues, "The same point may be made about British social policy more generally. Whether with respect to health, welfare, employment, or housing, Britain has self-consciously diminished the significance of race. Race plays only an inexplicit part in the policy-making calculus."

The point nonetheless remains that "a decent proportion of the 'special social need' aid . . . goes to authorities with large numbers of nonwhite students." There, "race is tacitly understood, but not mandated, to be such a 'social need.'"[50] In special programs of English-language instruction, for example, "nonwhites are the primary beneficiaries of language instruction, even though need, not race, is the predicate for this assistance."[51]

In short, the British practice is one of "doing good by doing stealth." Its central premise is that "race may be a predicate for positive policy, as long – and . . . only as long – as no one takes official notice of the fact."[52]

How well those policies are working is, of course, hard to determine. After all, the selfsame policy of inexplicitness precludes collecting and publishing data on some of the most crucial questions of educational attainment (for example, proportion of students, by race, continuing to A-level in secondary school or on to tertiary education).[53] But by some important sociological measures, things are getting better. In public opinion surveys taken between 1959 and 1975, the proportion of people saying that "feeling between white and coloured people is getting better" in Britain doubled, and the proportion saying it was getting worse halved.[54]

Just how transferable this British experience might be is, of course, an open question. "Benign neglect," when Daniel Patrick Moynihan proposed it to President Nixon as a solution to the American race problem, did not exactly fare well. Perhaps once the race card has been played, it simply cannot be recalled. Or perhaps the problem was simply that Moynihan's proposal was made public. As Kirp speculates, "Once exposed to bright light, benign neglect could not survive: this was a policy suggestion whose very existence depended upon

50   Ibid., p. 2.
51   Ibid., p. 105.
52   Ibid., p. 2.
53   Ibid., p. 106.
54   Ibid., pp. 111–12. This is to couch the advantages of "inexplicitness," once again, squarely in terms of avoiding counter-mobilization by opponents of those policies organized around distinctly immoral motives – "white backlash" in this instance. There might also be something to be said for the selfsame policy in terms of protecting the self-respect of the beneficiaries of the programs of special instruction.

circumspection."[55] Indeed, it seems only natural that a policy of inexplicitness cannot itself be explicitly announced.

> It makes good sense to attend to the racial dimension of a policy problem . . . by bringing nonwhites and whites together, at least so long as attention is not focused on the undertaking. That practice, familiar in the annals of both housing and schooling, is hard to defend logically; it is nonetheless right. If the ultimate end of public policy is to minimize the imposed salience of race while freeing individuals to choose for themselves what to make of their race, how better to proceed . . .? The teachers in Ealing forgot that the students who had been bused into their schools were nonwhite immigrants: what clearer measure of . . . success . . . could there be?[56]

Of course, whether the "policy of inexplicitness" deserves all the credit for these happy outcomes is a slightly open question. To sustain that sociological claim, we would need more evidence than (happily) we can have about the counterfactual – we would need evidence that, in the absence of inexplicitness, racial tensions would indeed have flared in the schools in Britain. Since the policy of inexplicitness was pursued, pretty consistently, pretty much from the start, evidence of that is sparse and indirect at best. But such as there is suggests that the policy of inexplicitness was indeed helpful in achieving morally superior outcomes. Here, as in the abortion case, it turns out to have been morally better to leave certain things unsaid.

That is offered as a reservation about arguments concerning the way in which free and open discussions – publicity, accountability and discursive defensibility – might serve to promote moral behavior. Sometimes, arguably, they do not. Sometimes, arguably, morally superior outcomes would have been produced by saying less, not more.

In a way, though, that proposition is more deeply subversive of my larger project. It is not just that there are some things that, morally, are better left unsaid. More to the point, we

55   Ibid., p. 109.
56   Ibid., pp. 130–1.

should not talk about those matters for fear of stirring things up politically. By going explicitly on a moral crusade, we invite moral counter-crusaders to enter the lists as well. An appearance of pragmatism might be the best way of pursuing truly principled objectives. But if that is true, then perhaps there is something wrong with my larger project of injecting morals into politics. Motivating moral behavior might, morally, be a bad idea. That is a theme to which the concluding chapters will at long last turn.

Conclusions

EIGHT

Infusing Morality Into Politics

In reaching toward conclusions, two issues arise on the basis of the foregoing. The first, to be addressed in this chapter, is how best to motivate moral behavior in politics. To foreshadow, my conclusion on that matter will be as follows. Previous chapters have revealed some more-or-less sneaky ways to motivate people to do things that are morally proper without necessarily doing them for self-consciously moralistic reasons. But the upshot of previous chapters is that, to some extent, appeals to self-consciously moral sentiments are always going to be required.

That conclusion raises a second question, though. Insofar as we must appeal to the self-consciously moral sentiments of people in order to motivate morally proper political actions, is it really such a good idea to infuse morality into politics in this way? Given the risks of counter-mobilization, might it be better on balance not even to try? That issue will be addressed in the final chapter.

The central problem that has been running throughout this book can be simply stated. What can we say to – what can we do to, or with – someone who asks, "Why should I be moral?" If someone is so lacking in any natural disposition to act morally as to ask the question in the first place, how can we induce such a person to act morally in the end?

Philosophers, no doubt, will leap to tell us that the question ("why should I be moral?") is simply ill formulated. From

Socrates' encounter with Thrysmachus forward, philosophers have been pointing out – in weary tones saved for the most tiresome students – that that query implicitly contains the seeds of its own solution. "Should" they will invariably say, is a morally-loaded word. Morality is just that set of things that you should do. So asking "why should I be moral?" is equivalent to asking "why should I do what I should do?" And to ask a question of that form is, of course, patently absurd. "QED," as philosophers would have it.

Such wholly abstract demonstration of timeless, contextless, analytic truths are not always wholly convincing, though. Such exercises seem akin to the analogous attempts of mathematical economists to seek truth while avoiding any serious confrontation with the real world. Those, as one of the more distinguished practitioners of that trade so aptly puts it, all too often amount to attempts to "extract the minimum of results from the minimum of assumptions."[1]

Clean models, abstracting from the peculiarities of particular cases, are indeed essential if we are ever to make sense of what is going on around us. But those models must then be reapplied to the real world, if they are ever to tell us what is really going on in the world around us, rather than just telling us what is going on inside the artificial world of the abstract model itself. That is what I hope to have been doing throughout: abstracting, but with a view to then reapplying the abstractions to a variety of actual social experiences. Story-telling it may be, but it is decidedly story-telling with a point.

Whatever philosophers may say, the real world is alas one in which the question "why should I be moral?" does indeed have resonance. Philosophers sometimes speak, metaphorically, of arguments being "forceful' or even of them being "compelling."[2] Would that they were. Philosophers themselves may regard the laws governing the logic of the "moral language game" as being strictly binding upon themselves. Ordinary people do not. Clever proofs and close logic-chopping simply get no motivational grip on people in the real world, very much more often than not.

To say that ordinary agents are not hyper-rational moral

1   Lancaster 1966, p. 132; cf. Sen 1977.
2   Nozick 1981, pp. 4–24.

logicians is not to say that they are wholly irrational either, though. There is a middle way between, on the one hand, hoping to persuade people via formal moral logic alone and, on the other hand, abandoning any hope of persuading them at all. I have been exploring several such "middle-way" strategies in the course of this book.

All of them assume that people are capable of being moved by moral argumentation, somehow or another, as I shall conclude. Equally, though, all of these strategies appreciate that not just any old argument will do the trick.[3] Our arguments must take certain forms, if they are to lock into people's motivational structures and move them to action.

A bstracting from the discussion of previous chapters, we can identify three broad styles of strategy for motivating moral behavior that have been recurring throughout the course of this book.

- First is a strategy of *"codetermination"* – so called because we can sometimes get people to behave better by showing them that much the same thought that motivates their belief that something is the morally right thing to do, in the first place, should also motivate them behaviorally to perform that action.
- Second is a strategy of *"ratcheting up"* from people's strong intuitions about the right thing to do in particular cases, generalizing them into principles that apply well beyond beyond those narrow intuitive applications.
- Third is a strategy of *"bridging down"* from people's general principles, showing how they actually commit them to specific acts in particular cases.

The first, "codetermination" strategy builds on the observation that motivation is needed in both parts of the moral enterprise. On the one side, there is the problem of how to motivate people to perform morally desirable actions: that is the problem which centrally concerned us here. But on the other side, we just as surely have to say something in order to motivate the belief that certain actions are indeed morally desirable: we have to say something to give people a reason to

3   Not even just any old argument, provided that it is a logically sound one.

believe that any particular act is indeed morally required of them, in the first place.[4] What underlies the "codetermination" strategy for motivating moral behavior is the thought that perhaps at least sometimes much the same reason people have for *believing* that an action is morally required of them will also lead them actually to *doing* whatever it is that morality demands.

Let us not overplay our hand here. For the story that we tell to persuade people that a certain act is morally required surely will, all too often, be wholly inappropriate as a story designed to persuade them to undertake that action. Hypotheticals and counterfactuals may be useful in persuading people what morality requires. Still, someone who remains genuinely puzzled as to "why should I be moral?" will remain wholly unmoved by such arguments.

Thus, we might ask people, "How would you feel if you were in their place?" or, "How would you feel if they did that to you?" To such classic questions, those who are genuinely morally unmotivated might cheerfully reply, "Happily, I'm not; and they won't."[5] To reply in that fashion is, of course, insistently to miss the point of the question. Complain though we may that such interlocutors verge on conversing in bad faith, we must nonetheless concede the literal truth of that rejoinder. A white Southerner is not going suddenly to turn black. It is hardly more likely that Ulster Catholics are going to gain political ascendancy in our lifetimes. All that just goes to show, I suppose, that motivation for moral beliefs and motiv-

---

4   Those sensitive to technicalities will detect the lack of perfect parallelism between "motivating the agent to do ø" on the one side, and "motivating within the agent the belief that ø" on the other. We cannot, strictly speaking, talk about "motivating the agent to believe," because motives are linked to voluntary acts whereas beliefs cannot strictly speaking be willed voluntarily. The parallel might therefore be better phrased as one between "giving someone a reason to believe ø" and "giving someone a reason to do ø."

5   Broad 1916. Dworkin 1977, p. 152. To return to the cases discussed in the opening pages of this book, neither Patrick Henry nor Thomas Jefferson would have been quite so blunt as to say, "No worries: there is no risk of blacks enslaving whites in Virginia during my lifetime, so I need not take any notice of the commands of the moral law as it applies to them." Still, in essence that is what they were saying: they saw the moral principles clearly enough; they just could not bring themselves to act in ways that they themselves acknowledged to be morally required.

ation for moral actions do not always necessarily travel together.

Still, at least occasionally, and perhaps much more than just occasionally, broadly the same story can be used to serve both purposes.[6] Indeed, Golden Rule ethics often do work precisely like that. In a world characterized by widespread tit-for-tat retaliation – in an arms race or a trade war or an extensive electorate, for example – you do unto others as you would have them do unto you, precisely because they will do unto you as you have done unto them.

There, motivation for believing that an action is morally correct and motivation for actually performing that action can sometimes spring from much the same source. What makes you think that the action is the morally correct one in the first place is the thought that you should do unto others as you would be done by. What actually gets you to perform that action, in a world of tit-for-tat retaliators, is the closely analogous thought that they will indeed do precisely as they have been done by.

The second set of strategies for motivating moral behavior is one which I have characterized, generically, as "ratcheting up" strategies. They start from the fact that people have certain firmly held moral intuitions. (The example I have used is the firm intuition that we have particularly strong obligations to take care of our own children.[7]) Such arguments then proceed to explore what sort of more general principles might underlie those bedrock intuitions, to show what further moral judgments follow from the systematic application of those principles that have been shown to underlie our firmly settled intuitions. Those propositions might strike us as counterintuitive. Still, we cannot shun them without, in effect, repudiating those bedrock moral judgments that we do adhere to and the deeper principles that can be found underlying them.

Thus, in that earlier book, I proceeded from our intuitions about our duty toward our own children to a conclusion about

6 "Broadly," because of course the Golden Rule asks you to do unto others as you *would* have others do unto you whereas the prudential tit-for-tat equivalent has you doing unto others as they *will* do unto you. For many commentators, the measure of morality lies precisely in the gap marked out by that counterfactual – the gap between what ethics requires of one, over and above what mere prudence would recommend.

7 Goodin 1985a, b.

our duty to help all the needy of the world, via a more general principle of "protecting the vulnerable."[8] In another application of broadly the same strategy, Gunnar Myrdal presented as the *American Dilemma*: either institute an effective regime of racial equality, or repudiate the American Creed and the norms of free and open dealings between equals that pervades so much of the rest of American life.[9]

As I have suggested in chapter 5, some such arguments might have motivated expansion of the franchise. Questions of consistency were forever being posed. How can we deny females what we readily grant otherwise identical males? How can we deny blacks what we readily grant otherwise identical whites? How can we deny a person the right to play a role in the civic life of their community at the ballot box when we are all too willing to allow him to play a role in its civic life at the battle front?

I suspect that this style of argument has considerable unexploited potential. There might be scope, along these lines, for mounting a potentially powerful argument about distributive justice, for example. The reasons we have – and, indeed, must have – for wanting to embrace norms of distributive justice at all might, this argument would suggest, go a long way toward fixing the content of those norms.[10] The argument for supposing that that might be so turns upon the following propositions:

1   (a) It is the essence of norms of justice that they serve as constraints upon the free play of "ordinary" distributional mechanisms; and
    (b) in societies like our own, ordinary distributions are determined according to market-based principles and institutions.
2   If norms of justice are going to get enough critical distance from market principles to provide this sort of constraint upon them, norms of justice cannot themselves simply consist in market principles at one remove.
3   Therefore, social justice cannot merely be a matter of respecting "freedom of choice" or "moral deserts" con-

8   Ibid.
9   Myrdal 1944, esp. chap. 1.
10   Goodin 1988a.

strued in narrowly market-based terms; understood in such ways, social justice would be simply incapable of doing that it is designed to do, which is to constrain markets.[11]

Various people will find fault with such an argument, to be sure. But whether or not this argument can ultimately be sustained, it can nonetheless usefully serve as yet another example of the way in which we might try to "ratchet up" from moral propositions that are widely embraced – principles about the function of norms of justice in any social system[12] – to propositions that are not so widely appreciated.

'Ratcheting up" is not always what is most needed, though. Sometimes we need instead to pursue the converse strategy for motivating moral behavior, "bridging down." That is to say, sometimes people want to do the right thing and they even know what the right thing is, in general or in the abstract. The problem is merely that they are uncertain what those general or abstract principles mean for particular cases; or perhaps their general disposition to "do the right thing" fails them in the face of temptations surrounding particular cases.

John Rawls's "veil of ignorance" is designed as a solution to the first sort of problem. Assuming we all want to be just and that we all agree that justice is essentially a matter of impartiality, the veil of ignorance (imagining we do not know who we are, what we have, or what we want) is a device to help us work out what particular institutions people committed to the

11 True, even Nozick (1974) would admit the necessity for constraining markets by enforcing tort and contract law. But the transfers by force and fraud which they prohibit themselves lie outside market principles; and if that is all our norms of justice rule out then they are not constraining market principles but are rather merely embodying them. Norms of justice that simply rewrite market principles (in terms of free choice, market-based moral deserts, tort and contract law) clearly cannot ever contravene market principles; and they therefore cannot do what norms of justice are supposed to do, which is to constrain by at least sometimes contravening our ordinary (market-based) distributive mechanisms.

12 Some, for example would deny that there is any widespread agreement on "the" function of norms of distributive justice. At some deeper level they are right, no doubt. But at the surface level they are surely wrong: whatever their deeper purposes, the way in which norms of distributive justice function (the way they work to serve those deeper purposes) is always and necessarily by constraining ordinary distributive mechanisms.

general principle of justice should choose.[13] "Constitutional-ism," as discussed in chapter 6, is the classic solution to the second sort of problem. Carving important general principles in stone makes it that much harder to rewrite them in the face of the temptations that inevitably arise in particular cases.

Each, however, is merely a different aspect of the same broad style of strategy for evoking moral motives. This third set of strategies can be characterized, generically, as devices to bring people's judgements about general principles forcefully to bear on their decisions about particular cases.

These, then, are the three more basic strategies of which all the more particular techniques discussed here are manifes-tations, in one way or another. And all of those strategies, in turn, implicitly assume that there is already something in people's motivational make-up – a "sense of morality" – to which we can appeal when trying to motivate moral beliefs and moral behavior.[14]

Nothing very fancy or very specific is meant by that term.[15] By it is meant merely that people have internalized notions of "right" and "wrong" and are, at least occasionally or at the margins, prepared to act upon them. There are many ways of interpreting the nature of the morality that they thus internal-ize and of describing what they are doing when judging actions "right" or "wrong." But whatever line we take on any of that, the simple fact remains that all of the strategies for motivating moral behavior discussed above require recourse to some such moral sense, in one way or another. In a way, that is to say no more than that in order to get a motivational grip on people there has to be something already within them for us to grip onto.

That is more transparently true of the second and third

---

13   Rawls 1971, sects 3, 4, and 24.
14   That old-fashioned term was recently revived by Rawls (1971, sect. 86).
15   Talk of a "moral sense" definitely does not necessarily commit us to a "cognitivist" – still less a "moral realist" – understanding of the nature of morality. The moral sense here in view does not necessarily deliver verdicts about true and false facts concerning moral realities that are fixed independently of any given human society. On the contrary, the moral sense here in view might be no more than the result of social conventions, with any uniformities across societies deriving from a broad uniformity of circumstances (Mackie 1977).

strategies than of the first, pehaps. In the second, "ratcheting up" case, people want to do the right thing, and they know what the right thing is at least in (some) particular cases. The motivational task, there, is first to show people what general principles underlie those particular judgments and then to show them what other right actions are required, under those same general principles.

In the third, "bridging down" case, people want to do the right thing, and they know what the right thing is in general or in the abstract. The motivational task, there, is to bring those abstract, general principles forcefully to bear upon particular cases, when people are uncertain of their application or infirm in their resolve.

In both those latter two cases, we are basically trying to take advantage of "the lag between our way of thought and our way of life."[16] In both cases, we are trying to get people to act upon principles which they are prepared both to espouse and even to act upon, at least for some purposes. In both cases, furthermore, those principles are self-consciously moral ones.

The need to appeal to people's sense of morality is less evident, perhaps, in the case of the first strategy. The crux of that "codetermination" case is that, there, people see the point but do not feel the force of moral argument.[17] The trick in motivating moral behavior, in that case, is to use broadly the same argument to motivate people to act on moral judgments as motivated them to recognize those as distinctively moral judgments in the first place.

Some of the examples I have given of how that might work, however, might rather seem to suggest that at least sometimes that can be accomplished without appealing directly to any moral principles that people themselves may have internalized. The threat of tit-for-tat retaliation, for example, provides purely prudential grounds for doing what the Golden Rule would require for more moralistic reasons. But even there, notice, we are counting on people's having some "sense of morality" sufficient to enable them to recognize their response to the

16 Kennedy 1955, p. 17.
17 Of course, some moral philosophers (e.g., Hare 1952) would deny the distinction: on such accounts, you just cannot see the point of morality without feeling its force. But that just amounts to another attempt at trying to provide a purely analytic solution to a genuine behavioral problem, of the sort spurned in the opening pages of this chapter.

question "how would you feel if they did that to you?" as providing an answer to a question of what morality might require of them. Only then would we be talking about a genuine case of "codetermination": a genuine case of the same thought leading the same person, at one and the same time, to recognize a course of action as being morally correct and to perform that course of action.

Even if some minimal appeal to this "sense of morality" is required in all three strategies, though, it is undeniably true that the second and third strategies need to make much greater use of it than does the first. And, within that pair, the third makes much greater demands on it than the second.

Characterized in those terms, the conclusions of the previous chapters can now be set out relatively succinctly.

1 The arguments given in connection with the discussions of reciprocity and extending the franchise in chapters 2 and 5 above suggest that we can go some considerable distance toward motivating moral behavior in politics by the first "codetermination" strategy alone.

2 For many of the most intellectually interesting an politically important cases, though, this first strategy will necessarily fail.

3 Ultimately, therefore, we must rely upon other strategies that depend upon people's having a relatively more robust sort of a "sense of morality" and a greater willingness to act upon it (however imperfect that might be) if we are to motivate them to behave morally in political affairs.

4 Fortunately, it seems that this condition is satisfied well enough and often enough for some combination of the second and third strategies to generate a good deal of moral behavior in a great many cases. That is the conclusion of evidence offered in Chapters 4, 6, and 7, in particular.[18]

5 Moral behavior is not automatically forthcoming, however. Given imperfections in people's sense of morality or in their willingness to act upon it, one or another of those strategies

18 This conclusion is supported by varous other sociological and social psychological writings on the subject, including, e.g.: Brandt 1976, esp. pp. 447–9; Etzioni 1988; and Mansbridge 1990.

really is required if we are to evoke anything like an adequate measure of moral behavior from them, politically.

Cynics may well scoff at this point, characterizing my thesis uncharitably as: "morality in, morality out." What I have been offering, they may say, is simply a way of motivating those predisposed to behave morally in the first place. And that, they may say, is not much of a trick at all.

In a way, such cynics would be right. Presumably, someone who already embraces the right general principles will be easier to move to act upon them than will someone who first needs to be shown what the right general principles really are – through, for example, a demonstration of the pattern that is revealed by his other, more particular moral choices. And someone who is prepared not only to acknowledge but also to act upon moral arguments, at least particular cases, is presumably less of a problem than is someone who knows what morality requires but sees that fact as providing no reason at all for performing that action.

Intellectually, the most exciting task is to find some way of getting this toughest nut in the moral vice. Politically, though, the most useful task may well be to find some better ways of securing rather more leverage on the less tough nuts. After all, they are the ones which can be cracked more easily. And, in any case, there may not be so many genuinely tough nuts in the population at large that we should worry overly much about them.

The political task here in view is, essentially, one of forming a broadly based coalition behind a certain range of recognizably moral policies. That being so, concentrating on the easiest recruits surely is the right strategy – at least wherever time and persuasive resources are at all scarce, as realistically they will almost always be. Hence I have, without apology, devoted at least as much attention to strategies which, while less intellectually exciting perhaps, are of more practical consequence.

NINE

Taking Morality Out
of Politics

This book has been concerned with motivating moral behavior in politics. Previous chapters pretty much assumed,
pretty much without argument, that that was a good thing to
do. Such an assumption comes naturally. Morality, after all,
is by definition the theory of the right and the good. If morality
is necessarily good, then motivating people to act upon it must
surely be good as well. That thought – or some subliminal
version of it – is what has allowed us to proceed this far
without any serious questioning of the larger project.

At this point, however, we must step back and ask the larger
question. It is, in any case, one which those coming to this
project from a background in politics or sociology rather than
of moral philosophy will probably have been asking from the
outset. Is it really such an indisputably good thing to motivate
people to act politically in such a morally principled way after
all?

It might not be. The proto-utilitarian anarchist William
Godwin took some satisfaction in being able to point out
that,

> Actions in the highest degree injurious to the public . . .
> have often proceeded from motives uncommonly con-
> scientious. The most determined political assassins . . .
> seem to have been deeply penetrated with anxiety for the
> eternal welfare of mankind. For these objects they sacri-
> ficed their ease, and cheerfully exposed themselves to

tortures and death. Benevolence probably had its part in lighting the fires of Smithfield, and pointing the daggers of Saint Bartholomew. The authors of the Gunpowder Treason were, in general, men remarkable for the sanctity of their lives, and the austerity of their manners.[1]

Or, for a more modern variation on this same basic theme, Barrington Moore comments upon how "the Sermon on the Mount can be a step on the road to the Inquisition, and the dream of a world without oppression become the justification for a terrorist secret police."[2] All of this is merely to say, in short, that moral motives are no guarantee of morally desirable outcomes.

The most casual reflection upon human history, ancient or modern, will reveal the catastrophic consequences that can sometimes come from infusing politics with moral principle.[3] Of course, any really big social movement admits of many causes and is consistent with still more theories; and really big crimes against humanity hold a very special fascination for social theorists. The upshot is that we know more – but understand less – about what really caused them, or how they might have been avoided.

But whatever might have been the leaders' deeper motives and the deeper sociological dynamics among their followers, nearly all of them operated – at the surface level, at least – in terms of an explicitly moral vision designed to justify their actions. Hitler and Stalin, Mao and Pol Pot all appealed, disingenuously or otherwise, to a moral vision in mounting

1 Godwin 1798, bk 2, chap. 4. For a more contemporary and homely example, consider Hare's (1981, p. 175) case of a physician fanatically committed to the principle of saving lives whatever the cost, which in his mind shows that "one may be fanatical about moral opinions even when they are sound."
2 Moore 1978, p. 399.
3 If the examples that follow – those of Hitler, Stalin, Mao, and Pol Pot – seem overly dramatic, consider the more mundane case, traced by Lijphart (1966, p. 288), of the way in which false pride and a symbolically-charged "moralism" led the Dutch to react to independence movements in the Dutch East Indies in a way that was damaging to the nation's strategic interests, economic prosperity, and international standing.

what would otherwise have been regarded as a straight-forwardly political sort of witchhunt.[4]

What exactly was the role of that moral appeal in garnering mass support for their causes is an open question. Sociologists have traditionally regarded it as mere rationalization, saying the true source of support for fascist and other such movements lay elsewhere – in the threat of "status deprivation" among marginal members of the middle classes, or some such.[5] More recent studies suggest that support for such movements might have been spread more evenly throughout the community and, more importantly for present purposes, might have been motivated by genuinely moral indignation and "cultural fundamentalism" at least as much as by material interests.[6]

Let us leave the sociology of the matter to the sociologists. What can nonetheless be safely inferred from these reports of their findings is this. Moralistic appeals may actually cause people to back the likes of Hitler; but whether or not they do that, such appeals certainly serve to *comfort* people in backing the likes of Hitler. That is to say, even if the true sociological dynamic lies elsewhere, moralistic arguments provide essential rationalizations that allow Hitler's supporters to live with themselves.

Were no such rationalizations available, at least some of those supporters might have felt much more guilty about the whole thing. That might have led, in at least some cases, to their calling an earlier halt to such disastrous episodes in human history. Even if moral appeals merely serve this more modest task of providing solace to the supporters of the likes of Hitler, that is more than enough to give us pause in our larger project of trying to infuse morality into politics.

4   Arendt 1966, Schwartz 1968. Apter 1987. Friedrich and Brzezinski 1956. Moodie (1975) discusses the Afrikaner civil religion in similar terms. On political witchhunts, see Bergesen 1977 and, for a more political interpretation, Goodin 1981.
5   Lasswell 1933. Lipset 1960, chaps 4 and 5.
6   Hamilton 1982. Wood and Hughes 1984. Thus, Barrington Moore (1978, p. 400) concludes that "sentiments of moral anger at felt injustices have been a powerful component" – if not the only or necessarily even the most important one – "in mass support of fascist movements."

One easy reply would be to distinguish, at this point, between the "true morality" which we hope to infuse into politics and the "pseudo-morality" upon which the political appeals of those infamous scoundrels relied. The counterexamples of Hitler and such like should not necessarily give us pause, this argument would go, because they were not really acting on moral principles – on *true* moral principles – at all. The fact that these reprobates lodged false claims under the banner of morality should not fool us, even if those claims might have fooled their followers.

Or, as an important variation on that theme, we might be protesting at the way in which moral principles, indisputably valid at the level of general principle, nonetheless get perverted politically in their applications to actual social problems. The way the principle is applied matters as much as its basic moral validity, of course. So infusing politics with even valid moral principles might not necessarily be a good idea, insofar as they are perverted in their application. Or, as yet another variation on the same basic theme, we might suppose that what is wrong with Hitler and such like is that they are acting on partial principles – true so far as they go, but representing only a subset of all true principles actually in play in the situation at hand.[7]

In all those variations, the objection is not to the infusion of moral principle into politics but rather against the infusion of *false* moral principles into politics. The problem is not that Hitler and such like are acting on moral principles. The problem is, instead, that they are acting on moral principles or interpretations of those principles that are either false or dangerously partial. Either way, the objection is not to the infusion of morality into politics: the objection is, rather, to the infusion of moral error into politics. Or so those keen to defend the infusion of morality to politics might say in response to the apparent counterexamples of Hitler, Stalin, Mao, and Pol Pot.

That reply really is just a little too easy, though. It makes it true that it is always good to act politically on moral principle, merely *by definition*. Whenever it would actually be bad politically to act from some principle, that is simply (re)defined as being an instance of acting upon a moral principle that is

7   That is how Hare (1981, chap. 10) would now choose to get around the problem of the "fanatic" he set for himself earlier (Hare 1963).

invalid or partial or incorrectly applied to the particular case at hand.

This strategy of making it true, by definition, that it is always good to act politically from moral principle is not just intellectually unsatisfying. It also poses genuine problems, on two levels. Philosophically, the ground shifts beneath our feet. Since those employing this device will in consequence never be prepared to say what *is* a true moral principle until after they see how it turns out in practice, they are never in a position to say in advance what morally we should do. Yet that is what we have always thought morality was supposed to do: to guide conduct.[8]

Connected to that is a second, system-design problem posed by such an approach. If we do not know what the right principles are until we see how they turn out, we can never set things up in such a way as to guarantee that the right principles are put into practice in the first place. That is to say, we cannot know what the right principle is until after things have played themselves out, at which time it is far too late to set things up so that the right principles get acted upon. People trying to design the system so that the right principles are put into effect will simply be chasing their own tails, if this line were adopted. The whole project of this book would become a logical impossibility, on that account.

Commentators dedicated to defending at all costs the proposition that it can never be a bad thing to infuse morality into politics might be nonetheless tempted by this line. But they will, in effect, be telling actors in the real world simply to do as they will and to let the chips fall where they may. The chips will indeed eventually fall; agents are not, on this account, excused from ultimate moral assessment. But since there is no

8 The artful dodger is not without a reply, at this point: he could simply say that we have always been wrong in thinking this, and that the point of morality is retrospective assessment of credit and blame rather than prospective guiding of action. But the reply lacks conviction. Surely many people would be prepared to see morality as having both sides to it. Few however could stomach one that had only the retrospective element. It would have us harking back, morally, to a system akin to primitive law's emphasis upon absolute, strict liability for damage done taking no account of foreseeability or hence fault. Again, many of us see some scope for strict liability rules in modern legal codes; few suppose there is no room at all for fault, however.

way of anticipating ahead of time how that assessment will actually turn out, there is no point worrying about it. People should just do what they will do regardless, and take the consequences as and when they come. And that, I take it, just *is* too easy a message. We are simply not prepared to believe that retrospective reckoning – without any hint of advance guidance at all – really is all there is to morality.

Such are the errors of this easy way of answering the challenge that infusing morality into politics might not be a good thing. I have expounded upon them at length merely because I want to use a variation on this argument myself, and in so doing I want to make sure to avoid committing the same errors.

At root, what is wrong with the too-easy version of the argument just canvassed is that it goes for too strong a claim, and rests it on too weak an assumption. Advocates of that line want to say that acting politically upon moral principle is *always* to the good; but in the end, that turns out to be true only *by definition*. And if that is how we are going to define true moral principles – as "working out for the best in the end" – then we will have no way of knowing ahead of time what we should do or try to get others to do.

I want to make a weaker claim, and to establish it in a stronger way. My claim is that acting upon moral principles in political life *usually* works out to the good. But my claim is not that that is true by definition alone. Unlike the argument canvassed above, I agree that we must have some independent standards of what morality requires of us. In saying that doing what they require usually works out for the best – that it usually does not lead to the Holocaust, or the Killing Fields, or whatever – I am therefore making an *empirical* claim, not an analytic one. Being a merely empirical claim, it can only be contingently (rather than necessarily) true. And that, in turn, means that it may well prove to be false – certainly in particular instances, and perhaps in general.

I hope and believe that that is not the case, though. There seem to be many good grounds for supposing that the sorts of moral principles I have been advocating – and still more the socio-political mechanisms I have been describing to get people to act upon those principles – will help to avoid Hitlerite excesses, rather than causing them. Indeed, it is virtually inconceivable that most of the mechanisms I have proposed could ever be turned to those sorts of ends.[9]

Of course, that sort of reply might not go very far toward allaying the fears of those who are horrified at the prospect of infusing moral principles into politics. But perhaps meeting their worries head-on is not the right response, anyway. To a large extent, we really are talking past one another. We are worrying about slightly different things, and responding to slightly different issues.

The most constructive step, at this point, would therefore be to set out as clearly as possible what is – and what is not – at stake on each side of the argument. Doing so will help us to join the issue squarely, insofar as there is indeed an issue to be joined. More than that, however, it will help us to see just to what a very large extent there is no issue standing between us to be joined at all.

What I have been proposing in this book is a set of mechanisms to help motivate people to act, politically, upon some very particular moral principles of a very standard sort. Those mechanisms are not guaranteed always to work perfectly; sometimes they will not work at all. But the fact that people might sometimes mistake or sometimes ignore the requirements of that moral code, even with my proposed mechanisms in place, ought not obscure this one very crucial fact. Insofar as those mechanisms infuse politics with morality at all, they infuse it with certain fairly specific (and really rather noncontentious) principles of morality.

Now, what those who look with horror upon the infusion of morality into politics fear seems to be something very different. What they fear is not the effects of any particular principles of morality – still less of my particular Golden Rule principles of morality. What they fear is, instead, the general effects of

9 That is to say, "inconceivable" – still less "*virtually* inconceivable" – is not equivalent to "impossible." There can be no guarantees that it will never happen: the mere fact that we cannot imagine it happening may mark a failure of imagination, rather than an objective impossibility. Political strategy is an essentially creative enterprise, and what new tricks remain yet to be discovered cannot be anticipated in advance. Thus, for my part, I should be suspicious of anyone who purports to be able to warrant that *anything* is impossible in politics.

"moralizing" politics, and the sorts of *attitudes* that that leads people to take toward their political opinions.

The fear is that people will come to regard most of their political opinions as if they were matters of high moral principle, whether or not they really are. The fear is that people will, in consequence, become increasingly adamant, inflexible, and intolerant even in the smallest matters of politics. The fear, most particularly, is that people's treating political opinions as if they were sacred values in this way will, from time to time, lead them to support the egregious excesses of a Hitler or a Stalin or a Mao or a Pol Pot. But even if matters stop well short of that, regarding political opinions as sacred values generates non-negotiable demands of a sort that ordinarily prove utterly intractable to ordinary political processes; and what cannot be settled by bargaining is left to be resolved by other, more bloody means.[10] Such are the fears of those who resist proposals to infuse morality into politics.

Notice, however, to what a large extent we really are talking past one another. They have no objection to the sorts of principles or mechanisms I am advocating, in particular; their objection is instead to the tendency toward inflexibility and intolerance that comes from introducing any sorts of moral principles into politics at all. I make no argument for supposing that those taking a moralistic attitude toward politics *should* be intolerant or inflexible. If anything, the general tendency of the Golden Rule ethic with which I have been working argues in precisely the opposite direction: for it, morality is first and foremost a system of mutual forbearances; and only by some fanatical perversion of that rule might it license moral absolutism of any sort.[11] So there really is a rather large scope for agreement between us. They have no objection to moralizing politics, so long as it does not lead to intolerance and inflexibility; and I have no reason for objecting to (and have some reason for actually insisting upon) that proviso myself.

The question at this point becomes simply one of whether we can find a sufficiently secure way of instituting a rule of tolerance to reassure those who are fearful that moralizing

---

10   Rose 1971, esp. chap. 14.
11   That is certainly what Hare (1981, chaps 5 and 10) would like to think. In this he is broadly supported by, e.g., Gewirth (1978).

politics might otherwise lead to intolerable excesses. I have a variety of proposals to make along these lines. Not all of them are that novel; and my analysis of how many of them might get a grip on people, motivationally, will by now be largely familiar as well.

The first proposal is just this. Perhaps we should try, insofar as possible, to rely upon mechanisms for motivating moral behavior that do not work through self-consciously moral agents. Some of the mechanisms I have been discussing, after all, make people behave morally without their doing so for moral reasons, necessarily. That is most obviously true of the way in which the tit-for-tat retaliation of simple reciprocity will force people to adopt Golden Rule practices of doing unto others as they would have others do unto them – not as a matter of morality, necessarily, so much as a matter of simple prudence. The same is true of the way in which uncertainty might work to make everyone imagine himself in the other's place – not as a matter of morality, again, so much as a matter of simple prudence (he might soon find himself in the other's place, after all). The point about these rules, in the present context, is just that they produce their morally desirable effects without working through morally self-conscious agents. If the objection to moralizing politics is that raising people's moral consciousness makes them more inflexible and intolerant, then those mechanisms of moralizing politics are immune to that objection. They produce their moralizing effects on the system without raising the self-consciousness – or hence inflexibility or intolerance levels – of the people at all.[12]

The question remains how we might set about making politics more moral than it would otherwise be, however. Naturally-occurring patterns of uncertainty or tit-for-tat retaliation might go some way toward forcing moral behavior upon people. But our project here is to find ways of further increasing that "baseline" level of morality in politics. And that, in turn, requires the intentional intervention of some morally self-conscious agents to pursue that moral goal. Who might they be, and how might we motivate them?

12 For those moral philosophers who would suppose that a good intention is the very essence of a moral action, this strategy of moralizing politics would not moralize it at all precisely because it works outside people's self-consciousness and intentions. But recall that I have, in chapter 1, argued that that cannot be the whole of morality.

The standard solution at this point – growing out of the example of "doing good by stealth," discussed at the end of chapter 7 – is to rely upon a more morally enlightened elite somehow restraining the intolerant impulses of the masses. Certainly survey research shows that elites express more support for values of political tolerance than do mass publics.[13] But in the end this solution to the problem raises more questions than it answers: specifically, "how is it that elites have come to have these values, themselves?" and "how is it that elites are capable of restraining genuinely intolerant masses in perpetuity?"

In the end, we have to conclude that elites are capable of being tolerant – practicing the "politics of accommodation" in a tolerant and even-handed way – if and only if the masses are prepared to allow them to do so. In Holland they are, or at least they were; in Ulster, they are not.[14] In the long term, there is nothing that elites can do in the face of genuinely intolerant followers.

Thus we are forced, ultimately, back to questions of how to make mass publics more tolerant – or, more precisely, how to tap their deeper, latent values in support of tolerance for purposes of more day-to-day political affairs. "Constitutionalism" is the standard solution here, and it is not a bad idea. As analyzed in chapter 6, the nature of a constitution is to force people to think in the long term rather than the short; and in the long term, their own position is far more uncertain than in the short. Hence they can be induced to accept principles – like toleration – as constitutional principles for the long haul, even when they might be tempted toward intolerant outbursts in the short run, on the grounds that the same principles that frustrate them today may well provide important protections for them some time later. People may even welcome these constitutional constraints upon their more ill-considered outbursts, reflecting as they do more "weakness of will" than considered judgments.

All this is by now familiar. I shall not elaborate further,

13 Stouffer 1955. Prothro and Grigg 1960. It is an open debate whether and to what extent mass publics are becoming more tolerant, although it is agreed by all parties to that debate that elites nonetheless remain more tolerant than mass publics. On all this, see: Sullivan, Piereson, and Marcus 1982; McClosky and Brill 1983; Sniderman et al. 1989.
14 Lijphart 1975 a, b. Rose 1971.

except to observe that in all the recent fervor to convene a national convention to amend the US Constitution (to ban abortion, or force balancing of the federal budget, or whatever), not one call has been heard for repeal of the First Amendment. Survey research may suggest that people are not much in favor of it. But given a chance, they do not seem very anxious to get rid of it either. That, in turn, might be taken as evidence – indirect and tentative though it may be – that people in their public capacities, reflecting upon long-term institutional arrangements, are prepared to behave more morally than their sporadic outbursts on the issues-of-the-day might lead us to fear.

I said right at the outset, at the end of chapter 1, that I was not going to be able to get the toughest nut in my moral vice. Only those with an internalized "sense of morality" already somehow within them will succumb to the sort of treatment that I have here been proposing. What may have seemed a major concession at the time has turned out to be less so than one might have feared, however.

Norms of non-exploitation are typically internalized, even by some otherwise morally pretty dubious characters. Most people seem willing to follow, in action as well as in thought, their principles to their logical conclusion. They are willing, for example, to extend the franchise to those who are, strictly speaking, politically or sociologically in no position to compel them to do so. People are willing to impose upon themselves the attitude of the "impartial spectator." They draft constitutions that they are then willing to live by, even once the tables have turned and their own interests are very differently served by them.

From all that we might reasonably infer that, even without cracking the toughest nut, there are more than enough materials with which we can work in attempting to motivate moral behavior in politics. Empirically, most people do indeed seem to internalize some basic sense of morality, to some extent or another. Politically, there seem to be plenty of ways of trying to hook into it – and to do so, almost certainly, for the good.

References

Ackerman, Bruce. 1980. *Social Justice and the Liberal State*. New Haven, Conn.: Yale University Press.

Ackerman, Bruce. 1984. The Storrs Lectures: Discovering the Constitution. *Yale Law Journal* 93: 1013–72.

Ackerman, Bruce. 1989a. Constitutional Politics/Constitutional Law. *Yale Law Journal* 99: 453–547.

Ackerman, Bruce. 1989b. Why Dialogue? *Journal of Philosophy* 86: 5–22.

Adams, Robert Merrihew. 1976. Motive Utilitarianism. *Journal of Philosophy* 73: 467–81.

Anon. 1987. Toward Consent and Cooperation: Reconsidering the Political Status of Indian Nations. *Harvard Civil Rights/Civil Liberties Law Review* 22: 509–622.

Anscombe, G. E. M. 1958. Modern Moral Philosophy. *Philosophy* 33: 1–19.

Anscombe, G. E. M. 1965. War and Murder. Pp. 45–62 in *Nuclear Weapons: A Catholic Response*, ed. Walter Stein. London: Merlin Press.

Apter, David E. 1987. Mao's Republic. *Social Research* 54: 691–729.

Arendt, Hannah. 1966. *The Origins of Totalitarianism*. 3rd edn. London: Allen & Unwin.

Arrow, Kenneth J. 1973. Some Ordinalist-Utilitarian Notes on Rawls's Theory of Justice. *Journal of Philosophy* 70: 245–63.

Arrow, Kenneth J. and Hurwicz, Leonid. 1972. An Optimality Criterion for Decision-Making Under Uncertainty. Pp. 1–11 in *Uncertainty and Expectations in Economics*, ed. C. F. Carter and J. L. Ford. Oxford: Blackwell.

Atkinson, A. B. 1990. Income Maintenance for the Unemployed in Britain and the Response to High Unemployment. *Ethics* 100: 569–85.

Atkinson, A. B. and Hills, John. 1989. *Social Security in Developed Countries: Are There Lessons for Developing Countries?* Discussion Paper WSP/38, Welfare State Programme. London: Suntory-Toyota International Centre for Economics and Related Disciplines, London School of Economics.

Axelrod, Robert. 1984. *The Evolution of Cooperation.* New York: Basic Books.

Bachrach, Michael. 1990. Commodities, Language and Desire. *Journal of Philosophy.* 87: 346–68.

Bachrach, Peter. 1967. *The Theory of Democratic Elitism.* Boston, Mass.: Little, Brown.

Bailey, Thomas A. 1944. *Woodrow Wilson and the Lost Peace.* New York: Macmillan.

Baldwin, Deborah. 1989. A Kinder, Gentler Agenda: Free Advice for the New President from Advocacy Groups. *Common Cause Magazine* 15 (1): 27–32.

Barr, Nicholas. 1987. *The Economics of the Welfare State.* London: Weidenfeld & Nicolson.

Barry, Brian. 1965. *Political Argument.* London: Routledge & Kegan Paul.

Barry, Brian. 1973. *The Liberal Theory of Justice.* Oxford: Clarendon Press.

Barry, Brian. 1978. Circumstances of Justice and Future Generations. Pp. 204–48 in *Obligations to Future Generations*, ed. Richard I. Sikora and Brian Barry. Philadelphia, Penn.: Temple University Press.

Barry, Brian. 1979. Justice as Reciprocity. Pp. 50–78 in *Justice*, ed. Eugene Kamenka and Alice E.–S. Tay. London: Edward Arnold.

Barry, Brian. 1989. *Theories of Justice.* Berkeley, Calif.: University of California Press.

Barsh, Russel L. and Henderson, James Youngblood. 1980. *The Road: Indian Tribes and Political Liberty.* Berkeley, Calif.: University of California Press.

Baumol, William J. 1965. *Welfare Economics and the Theory of the State.* London: George Bell & Sons.

Becker, Lawrence C. 1986. *Reciprocity.* London: Routledge & Kegan Paul.

Bendix, Reinhard and Rokkan, Stein. 1964. The Extension of Citizenship to the Lower Classes. Pp. 74–104 in Bendix, *Nation-Building and Citizenship.* New York: Wiley.

Benn, Stanley I. 1978. The Rationality of Political Man. *American Journal of Sociology* 83: 1271–6.

Bergesen, Albert James. 1977. Political Witch Hunts: The Sacred and the Subversive in Cross-National Perspective. *American Sociological Review* 42: 220–33.

Berman, Harold J. 1983. *Law and Revolution: The Formation of the*

Western Legal Tradition. Cambridge, Mass.: Harvard University Press.

Beveridge, William H. 1942. *Social Insurance and Allied Services*. Cmnd 6404. London: His Majesty's Stationery Office.

Bilmes, Jack M. 1979. The Evolution of Decisions in a Thai Village: A Quasi-Experimental Study. *Human Organization* 38: 169–78.

Blackstone, William, 1765. *Commentaries on the Laws of England*. London: Strahan.

Blackwell, Alice Stone. 1911. Objections Answered. Reprinted in NAWSA 1971.

Block, Fred; Cloward, Richard A.; Ehrenreich, Barbara; and Piven, Frances Fox. 1987. *The Mean Season: The Attack on the Welfare State*. New York: Pantheon.

Booth, Charles. 1892. *Pauperism and the Endowment of Old Age*. London: Macmillan.

Brams, Steven J. 1985. *Superpower Games*. New Haven, Conn.: Yale University Press.

Brandt, Richard B. 1976. The Psychology of Benevolence and Its Implications for Philosophy. *Journal of Philosophy* 73: 429–53.

Brennan, Geoffrey and Buchanan, James M. 1980. *The Power to Tax: Analytical Foundations of a Fiscal Constitution*. Cambridge: Cambridge University Press.

Brennan, Geoffrey and Buchanan, James M. 1985. *The Reason of Rules*. Cambridge: Cambridge University Press.

Brennan, Geoffrey and Pettit, Philip. 1990. Unveiling the Vote. *British Journal of Political Science* 20: 311–34.

Brewer, Daniel. 1908. Opinion of the U.S. Supreme Court. *Muller v. Oregon*. 208 U.S. 416–23.

Broad, C. D. 1916. On the Function of False Hypotheses in Ethics. *International Journal of Ethics* (now *Ethics*) 26: 377–97.

Brock, Michael. 1973. *The Great Reform Act*. London: Hutchinson.

Brown, Stuart M. 1955. Inalienable Rights. *Philosophical Review* 64: 192–211.

Bryce, James. 1901. Flexible and Rigid Constitutions. 145–254 in Bryce, *Studies in History and Jurisprudence*, Vol. 1. Oxford: Oxford University Press.

Buchanan, James M. 1987. The Constitution of Economic Policy. Stockholm: The Nobel Foundation. Reprinted in: *Science* 236 (1987): 1433–6; and *American Economic Review* 77 (1987): 243–50.

Buchanan, James M. and Tullock, Gordon. 1962. *The Calculus of Consent*. Ann Arbor, Mich.: University of Michigan Press.

Calabresi, Guido. 1982. *A Common Law for the Age of Statutes*. Cambridge, Mass.: Harvard University Press.

Calhoun, John C. 1853. *A Disquisition on Government*, ed. C. Gordon Post. Indianapolis, Ind.: Bobbs-Merrill, 1953.

Conybeare, John. 1986 Trade Wars: A Comparative Study of Anglo-Hanse, Franco-Italian and Hawley-Smoot Conflicts. Pp. 147–72 in *Co-operation Under Anarchy*, ed. Kenneth A. Oye. Princeton, NJ: Princeton University Press.

Corwin, Edward S. 1928–9. The Higher Law Background of American Constitutional Law. *Harvard Law Review* 42: 149–85, 365–409.

Cover, Robert M. 1988. Social Security and Constitutional Entitlement. Pp. 69–87 in *Social Security: Beyond the Rhetoric of Crisis*, ed. Theodore R. Marmor and Jerry L. Mashaw. Princeton, NJ: Princeton University Press.

Cutright, Phillips. 1965. Political Structure, Economic Development and National Social Security Programs. *American Journal of Sociology* 70: 537–50.

Davidson, Donald. 1963. Actions, Reasons and Causes. *Journal of Philosophy* 60: 685–700.

Davidson, Donald. 1969. How is Weakness of the Will Possible? Pp. 93–113 in *Moral Concepts*, ed. Joel Feinberg. Oxford: Oxford University Press.

Dawes, R.; McTavish, J.; and Shaklee, H. 1977. Behavior, Communications and Assumptions about Other People's Behavior in a Commons Dilemma Situation. *Journal of Personality and Social Psychology* 35: 1–35.

Day, Patricia and Klein, Rudolph. 1987. *Accountabilities: Five Public Services*. London: Tavistock.

Destler, I. M. 1978. United States Food Policy 1972–1976: Reconciling Domestic and International Objectives. *International Organization* 32: 617–53.

Dicey, A. V. 1908. *The Law of the Constitution*. 7th edn. London: Macmillan.

Downing, Brian M. 1989. Medieval Origins of Constitutional Government in the West. *Theory and Society* 18: 213–47.

Downs, Anthony. 1960. Why the Government Budget Is Too Small in a Democracy. *World Politics* 12: 541–63.

Dryzek, John S. 1990. *Discursive Democracy*. Cambridge: Cambridge University Press.

Dryzek, John S. and Goodin, Robert E. 1986. Risk-Sharing and Social Justice: The Motivational Foundations of the Post-War Welfare State. *British Journal of Political Science* 16: 1–34. Reprinted in Goodin, Le Grand, et al. 1987, pp. 37–73.

Duchacek, Ivo D. 1973. *Power Maps: Comparative Politics of Constitutions*. Santa Barbara, Calif.: ABC-Clio.

Duncan, Greg J. 1984. *Years of Poverty, Years of Plenty*. Ann Arbor, Mich.: Survey Research Center, Institute for Social Research, University of Michigan.

Duncan, Greg J.; Hill, Martha S.; Hoffman, Saul D. 1988. Welfare Dependence Within and Across Generations. *Science* 239: 467–71.

Dworkin, Ronald M. 1977. *Taking Rights Seriously*. London: Duckworth.

Edgeworth, Francis Y. 1897. The Pure Theory of Taxation. Pp. 119–36 in *Classics in the Theory of Public Finance*, ed. Richard A. Musgrave and Alan T. Peacock. London: Macmillan, 1967.

Elster, Jon. 1978. Exploring Exploitation. *Journal of Peace Research* 15: 3–17.

Elster, Jon. 1984. *Ulysses and the Sirens*. Revised edn. Cambridge: Cambridge University Press. Original edn 1979.

Elster, Jon. 1986. The Market and the Forum: Three Varieties of Political Theory. Pp. 103–32 in *Foundations of Social Choice Theory*, ed. Jon Elster and Aanund Hylland. Cambridge: Cambridge University Press.

Elster, Jon. 1988. Introduction. Pp. 1–18 in *Constitutionalism and Democracy*, ed. Jon Elster and Rune Slagstrad. Cambridge: Cambridge University Press.

Etzioni, Amitai. 1967. The Kennedy Experiment. *Western Political Quarterly* 20: 361–80.

Etzioni, Amitai. 1988. *The Moral Dimension: Toward a New Economics*. New York: Free Press.

Feinberg, Joel. 1980. *Rights, Justice and the Bounds of Liberty*. Princeton, NJ: Princeton University Press.

Ferejohn, John A. 1974. *Pork Barrel Politics: Rivers and Harbors Legislation, 1947–68*. Stanford, Calif.: Stanford University Press.

Field, Elizabeth B. 1988. Free and Slave Labor in the Antebellum South: Perfect Substitutes or Different Inputs? *Review of Economics and Statistics* 70: 654–9.

Fiss, Owen A. 1984. Against Settlement. *Yale Law Journal* 93: 1073–91.

Fisse, Brent and Braithwaite, John. 1983. *The Impact of Publicity on Corporate Offenders*. Albany, NY: State University of New York Press.

Friedrich, Carl J. 1964. *Transcendent Justice: The Religious Dimension of Constitutionalism*. Durham, NC: Duke University Press.

Friedrich, Carl J. 1968. *Constitutional Government and Democracy*. 4th edn. Waltham, Mass.: Ginn & Co.

Friedrich, Carl J. 1974. *Limited Government*. Englewood Cliffs, NJ: Prentice-Hall.

Friedrich, Carl J. and Brzezinski, Zbigniew K. 1956. *Totalitarian Dictatorship and Autocracy*. Cambridge, Mass.: Harvard University Press.

Fudenberg, Drew and Kreps, David M. 1989. Reputation in the Simultaneous Play of Multiple Opponents. *Review of Economic Studies* 54: 541–68.

Fuller, Lon L. 1969. *The Morality of Law*. 2nd edn. New Haven, Conn.: Yale University Press.

Genn, Hazel. 1987. *Hard Bargaining: Out of Court Settlement in Personal Injury Actions*. Oxford: Clarendon Press.

Genovese, Eugene D. 1974. *Roll, Jordan, Roll: The World the Slaves Made*. New York: Vintage Books, Random House.

Gewirth, Alan. 1978. *Reason and Morality*. Chicago, Ill.: University of Chicago Press.

Godwin, William, 1798. *Enquiry Concerning Political Justice*. 3rd edn. Harmondsworth, Middx: Penguin, 1976.

Goodin, Robert E. 1976. *The Politics of Rational Man*. London: Wiley.

Goodin, Robert E. 1980. *Manipulatory Politics*. New Haven, Conn.: Yale University Press.

Goodin, Robert E. 1981. Civil Religion and Political Witchhunts: Three Explanations. *Comparative Politics* 14: 1–16.

Goodin, Robert E. 1982. *Political Theory and Public Policy*. Chicago, Ill.: University of Chicago Press.

Goodin, Robert E. 1985a. *Protecting the Vulnerable: A Re-Analysis of Our Social Responsibilities*. Chicago, Ill.: University of Chicago Press.

Goodin, Robert E. 1985b. Vulnerabilities and Responsibilities: An Ethical Defense of the Welfare State. *American Political Science Review* 79: 775–87.

Goodin, Robert E. 1986. Laundering Preferences. Pp. 75–102 in *Foundations of Social Choice Theory*, ed. Jon Elster and Aanund Hylland. Cambridge: Cambridge University Press.

Goodin, Robert E. 1988a. Markets: Their Morals and Ours. *Australian Society (Supplement)* 7(12): 7–9.

Goodin, Robert E. 1988b. *Reasons for Welfare: The Political Theory of the Welfare State*. Princeton, NJ: Princeton University Press.

Goodin, Robert E. 1989. Do Motives Matter? *Canadian Journal of Philosophy* 19: 405–20.

Goodin, Robert E. 1990a. Government House Utilitarianism. Pp. 140–60 in *The Utilitarian Response*, ed. Lincoln Allison. London: Sage.

Goodin, Robert E. 1990b. Stabilizing Expectations: The Role of Earnings-Related Benefits in Social Welfare Policy. *Ethics* 100: 530–53.

Goodin, Robert E.; Le Grand, Julian; et al. 1987. *Not Only the Poor: The Middle Classes and the Welfare State*. London: Allen & Unwin.

Gouldner, Alvin W. 1960. The Norm of Reciprocity. *American Sociological Review* 25: 161–78.

Gowing, Margaret. 1975. Obituary Notice: Richard Titmuss. *Proceedings of the British Academy* 51: 401–28.

Gregg, Gail. 1981. "Let Us Act Together" Reagan Exhorts Congress. *Congressional Quarterly Weekly Report* 39 (8): 331–5.

Greider, William. 1981. *The Education of David Stockman and Other Americans*. New York: E. P. Dutton.

Grey, Thomas C. 1979. Constitutionalism: An Analytic Framework. Pp. 189–209. in *Nomos XX: Constitutionalism*, ed. J. R. Pennock and J. W. Chapman. New York: New York University Press.

Griffith, John, ed. 1983. *Socialism in a Cold Climate*. London: Unwin.

Habermas, Jürgen. 1964/1974. The Public Sphere, trans. S. & F. Lennox. *New German Critique* 3: 49–55.

Habermas, Jürgen. 1973. *Legitimation Crisis* trans. Thomas McCarthy. Oxford: Polity Press, 1988.

Hamilton, Alexander; Madison, James; and Jay, John. 1788. *The Federalist*, ed. Jacob E. Cooke. Middletown, Conn.: Wesleyan University Press, 1961.

Hamilton, Richard. 1982. *Who Voted for Hitler?* Princeton, NJ: Princeton University Press.

Hanson, Russell L. 1987. The Expansion and Contraction of the American Welfare State. In Goodin, Le Grand, et al. 1987, pp. 169–99.

Hardin, Russell. 1982. Exchange Theory on Strategic Bases. *Social Science Information* 21: 251–72.

Hardin, Russell. 1988. *Morality within the Limits of Reason*. Chicago, Ill.: University of Chicago Press.

Hare, R. M. 1952. *The Language of Morals*. Oxford: Clarendon Press.

Hare, R. M. 1963. *Freedom and Reason*. Oxford: Clarendon Press.

Hare, R. M. 1973. Rawls's Theory of Justice. *Philosophical Quarterly* 23: 144–55, 241–52.

Hare, R. M. 1981. *Moral Thinking*. Oxford: Clarendon Press.

Harman, Gilbert. 1975. Moral Relativism Defended. *Philosophical Review* 84: 3–22.

Harrison, Brian. 1978. *Separate Spheres: The Opposition to Women's Suffrage in Britain*. London: Croom Helm.

Harsanyi, John C. 1953. Cardinal Utility in Welfare Economics and in the Theory of Risk-Taking. *Journal of Political Economy* 61: 434–5.

Harsanyi, John C. 1955. Cardinal Welfare, Individualistic Ethics and Interpersonal Comparisons of Utility. *Journal of Political Economy* 63: 309–21.

Harsanyi, John C. 1982. Morality and the Theory of Rational Behaviour. Pp. 39–62 in *Utilitarianism and Beyond*, ed. Amartya Sen and Bernard Williams. Cambridge: Cambridge University Press.

Hart, H. L. A. 1955. Are There Any Natural Rights? *Philosophical Review* 64: 175–91.

Hart, H. L. A. 1961. *The Concept of Law*. Oxford: Clarendon Press.

Hayter, Teresa. 1981. *The Creation of World Poverty: An Alternative View to the Brandt Report*. London: Pluto Press.

Heclo, Hugh. 1981. Towards a New Welfare State? Pp. 383–406 in

The Development of Welfare States in Europe and America, ed. Peter Flora and Arnold J. Heidenheimer. New Brunswick, NJ: Transaction Books.

Heidenheimer, Arnold J., ed. 1970. *Political Corruption*. New York: Holt Rinehart & Winston.

Hirschman, Albert O. 1991. *The Rhetoric of Reaction*. Cambridge, mass.: Harvard University Press.

Hobsbawm, E. J. 1985. *Bandits*. 2nd edn. Harmondsworth, Mddx: Penguin.

Hochschild, Jennifer L. 1988. Race, Class, Power, and the American Welfare State. Pp. 157–84 in *Democracy and the Welfare State*, ed. Amy Gutmann. Princeton, NJ: Princeton University Press.

Hofstadter, Richard. 1948. *The American Political Tradition and the Men Who Made It*. New York: Vintage Books, Knopf.

Holmes, Stephen. 1988. Gag Rules, or the Politics of Omission. Pp. 19–58 in *Constitutionalism and Democracy*, ed. Jon Elster and Rune Slagstad. Cambridge: Cambridge University Press.

Hooker, Richard. 1648. *On the Laws of Ecclesiastical Polity*, ed. A. S. McGrade. Cambridge: Cambridge University Press, 1989.

Hume, David. 1739. *A Treatise of Human Nature*. London: John Noon.

Hume, David. 1777. *An Enquiry Concerning the Principles of Morals*. London: Cadell.

Johnson, Nevil. 1974. Defining Accountability. *Public Administration Bulletin* 17: 3–13.

Kagan, Robert A. 1978. *Regulatory Justice: Implementing a Wage-Price Freeze*. New York: Russell Sage Foundation.

Kahneman, Daniel; Knetsch, Jack L.; Thaler, Richard H. 1986a. Fairness and the Assumptions of Economics. *Journal of Business* 59 (Supplement): S285–S300.

Kahneman, Daniel; Knetsch, Jack L.; and Thaler, Richard H. 1986b. Fairness as a Constraint on Profit Seeking: Entitlements in the Market. *American Economic Review* 76: 728–41.

Kahneman, Daniel; Slovic, Paul; and Tversky, Amos, eds. 1982. *Judgment Under Uncertainty: Heuristics and Biases*. Cambridge: Cambridge University Press.

Kahneman, Daniel and Tversky, Amos. 1979. The Simulation Heuristic. In Kahneman , Slovic, and Tversky 1982, pp. 200–8.

Kant, Immanuel. 1785. *Foundations of the Metaphysics of Morals*, trans. L. W. Beck. Chicago, Ill.: University of Chicago Press, 1949.

Kant, Immanuel. 1795. Perpetual Peace . Pp. 93–130 in *Kant's Political Writings*, trans. H. B. Nisbet, ed. Hans Reiss. Cambridge: Cambridge University Press, 1970.

Kaufman, Herbert. 1976. *Are Government Organizations Immortal?* Washington, DC: Brookings Institution.

Keech, William R. 1968. *The Impact of Negro Voting*. Chicago, Ill.: Rand McNally.

Keillor, Garrison. 1991. Taking the C Train. *Guardian Weekly* 144 (#1: 6 January): 17.

Kennedy, John F. 1955. *Profiles in Courage*. New York: Harper.

Key, V. O., Jr. 1949. *Southern Politics*. New York: Knopf.

Keynes, John Maynard. 1937. The General Theory of Employment. *Quarterly Journal of Economics* 51: 209–23.

Kirchheimer, Otto. 1969. *Politics, Law and Social Change*, ed. F. S. Burin and K. L. Shell. New York: Columbia University Press.

Kirp, David L. 1979. *Doing Good by Doing Little: Race and Schooling in Britain*. Berkeley, Calif.: University of California Press.

Kreps, David M. and Wilson, Robert. 1982. Reputation and Imperfect Information. *Journal of Economic Theory* 27: 253–79.

Lakoff, George and Johnson, Mark. 1980. *Metaphors We Live By*. Chicago, Ill.: University of Chicago Press.

Lancaster, Kelvin J. 1966. A New Approach to Consumer Theory. *Journal of Political Economy* 74: 132–57.

Lasswell, Harold. 1933. The Psychology of Hitlerism. *Political Quarterly* 4: 373–84.

Le Grand, Julian. 1982. *The Strategy of Equality*. London: Allen & Unwin.

Lijphart, Arend. 1966. *The Trauma of Decolonization: The Dutch and West New Guinea*. New Haven, Conn.: Yale University Press.

Lijphart, Arend. 1975a. *The Politics of Accommodation: Pluralism and Democracy in the Netherlands*. 2nd edn. Berkeley, Calif.: University of California Press.

Lijphart, Arend. 1975b. Review Article: The Northern Ireland Problem: Cases, Theories and Solutions. *British Journal of Political Science* 5: 83–106.

Lijphart, Arend. 1977. *Democracy in Plural Societies*. New Haven, Conn.: Yale University Press.

Lindahl, Erik. 1960. Tax Principles and Tax Policies. *International Economic Papers* 10: 7–23.

Lipset, Seymour Martin. 1960. *Political Man*. New York: Doubleday.

Lipsey, Richard G. and Lancaster, Kelvin J. 1956. The General Theory of Second Best. *Review of Economic Studies* 24: 11–33.

Locke, John. 1690. *Second Treatise of Government*, ed. Peter Laslett. Cambridge: Cambridge University Press, 1960.

Lowenstein, Karl, 1938. Legislative Control of Political Extremism in European Democracies. *Columbia Law Review* 38: 591–622 , 725–74.

Luban, David. 1988. *Lawyers and Justice: An Ethical Study*. Princeton, NJ: Princeton University Press.

Luker, Kristen. 1984. *Abortion and the Politics of Motherhood*. Berkeley, Calif.: University of California Press.

Maass, Arthur. 1951. *Muddy Waters*. Cambridge, Mass.: Harvard University Press.

McCloskey, Herbert and Brill, Alida. 1983. *Dimensions of Tolerance*. New York: Russell Sage Foundation.

McIlwain, Charles Howard. 1947. *Constitutionalism: Ancient & Modern*. Revised edn. Ithaca, NY: Cornell University Press.

Mackie, J. L. 1977. *Ethics: Inventing Right and Wrong*. Harmondsworth, Mddx: Penguin.

Maddox, Graham. 1989. Constitution. Pp. 50–67 in *Political Innovation and Conceptual Change*, ed. T. Ball, J. Farr, and R. L. Hanson. Cambridge: Cambridge University Press.

Madison, James. 1787. *Notes of Debates in the Federal Convention of 1787*, ed. Adrienne Koch. New York: Norton, 1967.

Maine, Henry Sumner. 1885. *Popular Government*. London: John Murray.

Maley, Yon. 1987. The Language of Legislation. *Language in Society* 16: 25–48.

Mansbridge, Jane J., ed. 1990. *Beyond Self-Interest*. Chicago, Ill.: University of Chicago Press.

Margolis, Julius, 1955. A Comment on the Pure Theory of Public Expenditure. *Review of Economics and Statistics* 37: 347–9.

Marshall, John. 1831. Opinion of the U.S. Supreme Court. *Cherokee Nation v. Georgia*. 5 Peters (30 U.S.) 1–20.

Mathews, Donald R. 1960. *U.S. Senators and Their World*. Chapel Hill, NC: University of North Carolina Press.

Mathews, Stanley. 1886. Opinion of the U.S. Supreme Court. *Choctaw Nation v. United States*. 119 U.S. 25–41.

May, Ernest. 1971. *The Law, Privileges, Proceedings and Usage of Parliament*, ed. B. Cocks. 18th edn. London: Butterworth.

May, Kenneth O. 1952. A Set of Independent, Necessary and Sufficient Conditions for Simple Majority Decision. *Econometrica* 20: 680–4.

Midgaard, Knut. 1980. On the Significance of Language and a Richer Concept of Rationality. Pp. 83–97 in *Politics as Rational Action*, ed. Leif Lewin and Evert Vedung. Dordrecht, Holland: Reidel.

Midgaard, Knut; Stenstadvold, Halvor; and Underdal, Arild. 1973. An Approach to Political Interlocutions. *Scandinavian Political Studies* 8: 9–36.

Milgrom, Paul R.; North, Douglass C.; and Weingast, Barry R. 1990. The Role of Institutions in the Revival of Trade: The Law Merchant, Private Judges and the Champagne Fairs. *Economics and Politics* 2: 1–24.

Milgrom, Paul and Roberts, John. 1982. Predation, Reputation and Entry Deterrence. *Journal of Economic Theory* 27: 280–312.

Mill, John Stuart. 1859. *On Liberty*. Pp. 5–141 in *John Stuart Mill: Three Essays*, ed. Richard Wollheim. Oxford: Clarendon Press, 1975.

Mill, John Stuart. 1861. *Considerations on Representative Government*. Pp. 142–423 in *John Stuart Mill: Three Essays*, ed. Richard Wollheim. Oxford: Clarendon Press, 1975.

Mill, John Stuart. 1869. *The Subjection of Women*. Pp. 425–58 in *John Stuart Mill: Three Essays*, ed. Richard Wollheim. Oxford: Clarendon Press, 1975.

Miller, Samuel F. 1885. Opinion of the U.S. Supreme Court. *United States v. Kagama*. 118 U.S. 375–85.

Milnor, John. 1954. Games Against Nature. Pp. 49–59 in *Decision Processes*, ed. R. M. Thrall, C. H. Coombs, and R. L. Davis. New York: Wiley.

Monore, Kristen; Barton, Michael C.; and Klingemann, Ute. 1991. Altruism and the Theory of Rational Action: An Analysis of Rescuers of Jews in Nazi Europe. *Ethics* 101: 103–22.

Montesquieu, C. L. de. 1748. *The Spirit of the Laws*, trans. Thomas Nuget. New York: Hafner Press, Macmillan, 1949.

Moodie, T. Dunbar. 1975. *The Rise of Afrikanerdom: Power, Apartheid, and the Afrikaner Civil Religion*. Berkeley, Calif.: University of California Press.

Moore, Barrington, Jr. 1970. *Reflections on the Causes of Human Misery*. Boston, Mass.: Beacon Press.

Moore, Barrington, Jr. 1978. *Injustice: The Social Bases of Obedience and Revolt*. London: Macmillan.

Musgrave, Richard A. 1974. Maximin, Uncertainty and the Leisure Trade-Off. *Quarterly Journal of Economics* 88: 625–32.

Musgrave, Richard A. 1976. ET, OT and SBT. *Journal of Public Economics* 6: 3–16.

Myrdal, Gunnar. 1944. *An American Dilemma*. New York: Harper & Row.

Nagel, Thomas. 1970. *The Possibility of Altruism*. Oxford: Clarendon Press.

Nagel, Thomas. 1989. What Makes a Political Theory Utopian? *Social Research* 56: 903–20.

NAWSA (National American Woman Suffrage Association). 1971. *Woman Suffrage: Arguments and Results, 1910–11*. New York: Kraus Reprint Co.

Nozick, Robert. 1974. *Anarchy, State and Utopia*. Oxford: Blackwell.

Nozick, Robert. 1981. *Philosophical Explanations*. Cambridge, Mass.: Harvard University Press.

Olson, Mancur, Jr. 1965. *The Logic of Collective Action*. Cambridge, Mass.: Harvard University Press.

Orbell, John M.; von de Kragt, Alphons J. C.; and Dawes, Robyn M.

1988. Explaining Discussion-induced Cooperation. *Journal of Personality and Social Psychology* 54: 811–19.

Parry, Geraint. 1969. *Political Elites*. London: Allen & Unwin.

Pateman, Carole. 1988. *The Sexual Contract*. Oxford: Polity Press.

Pateman, Carole. 1990. Promise and Paradox: Women and Democratic Citizenship. The York Lecture, York University, Ont., delivered 23 October 1990.

Patterson, Orlando. 1982. *Slavery and Social Death: A Comparative Study*. Cambridge Mass.: Harvard University Press.

Pennock, J. R. and Chapman, J. W., eds. 1979. *Nomos XX: Constitutionalism*. New York: New York University Press.

Pettit, Philip. 1982. Habermas on Truth and Justice. Pp. 207–28 in *Marx and Marxisms*, ed. G. H. R. Parkinson. Cambridge: Cambridge University Press for the Royal Institute of Philosophy.

Pigou, A. C. 1932. *The Economics of Welfare*. 4th edn. London: Macmillan.

Pocock, J. G. A. 1957. *The Ancient Constitution and the Feudal Law*. Cambridge: Cambridge University Press.

Postema, Gerald J. 1989. Bentham on the Public Character of Law. *Utilitas* 1: 41–61.

Prothro, James W. and Grigg, Charles M. 1960. Fundamental Principles of Democracy: Bases of Agreement and Disagreement. *Journal of Politics* 22: 276–94.

Rae, Douglas W. 1969. Decision-Rules and Individual Values in Constitutional Choice. *American Political Science Review* 63: 40–56.

Ransom, Roger L. and Sutch, Richard. 1977. *One Kind of Freedom: The Economic Consequences of Emancipation*. Cambridge: Cambridge University Press.

Rawls, John. 1958. Justice as Fairness. *Philosophical Review* 67: 164–94.

Rawls, John. 1963. The Sense of Justice. *Philosophical Review* 72: 281–305.

Rawls, John. 1967. Legal Obligation and the Duty of Fair Play. Pp. 3–18 in *Law and Philosophy*, ed. Sidney Hook. New York: New York University Press.

Rawls, John. 1971. *A Theory of Justice*. Cambridge, Mass.: Harvard University Press.

Rawls, John. 1977. The Basic Structure as Subject. *American Philosophical Quarterly* 14: 159–65.

Rawls, John. 1985. Justice as Fairness: Political Not Metaphysical. *Philosophy and Public Affairs* 14: 223–51.

Rawls, John. 1987. The Idea of an Overlapping Consensus. *Oxford Journal of Legal Studies* 7: 1–25.

Reagan, Ronald. 1981a. Address to a Joint Session of Congress: February 18, 1981. *Congressional Quarterly Weekly Report* 39 (8): 360–3.

Reagan, Ronald. 1981b. Budget Message to Congress, Transmitted March 10, 1981. *Congressional Quarterly Weekly Report* 39 (11): 485.

Riker, William H. 1962. *The Theory of Political Coalitions*. New Haven, Conn.: Yale University Press.

Rochester Woman's Rights Convention. 1848. Proceedings of the Woman's Rights Convention, Held at the Unitarian Church, Rochester, NY, August 2, 1848, to Consider the Rights of Woman, Politically, Religiously and Industrially. In *Woman's Rights Conventions, Seneca Falls & Rochester, 1848*. New York: Arno & the New York Times, 1969.

Rogin, Michael Paul. 1971. Liberal Society and the Indian Question. *Politics & Society* 1: 269–312.

Rogowski, Ronald. 1974. *Rational Legitimacy*. Princeton, NJ: Princeton University Press.

Rose, Richard. 1971. *Governing Without Consensus*. London: Faber & Faber.

Rose, Richard. 1976a. On the Priorities of Citizenship in the Deep South and Northern Ireland. *Journal of Politics* 38: 247–91.

Rose, Richard. 1976b. On the Priorities of Government: A Developmental Analysis of Public Policies. *European Journal of Political Research* 4: 247–89.

Rousseau, Jean-Jacques. 1762. *Social Contract*, trans. G. D. H. Cole. London: Dent, 1913.

Safire, William. 1978. *Safire's Political Dictionary*. New York: Ballantine Books.

Samuelson, Paul A. 1954. The Pure Theory of Public Expenditure. *Review of Economics & Statistics* 36: 387–9.

Sartori, Giovanni. 1962. Constitutionalism: A Preliminary Discussion. *American Political Science Review* 56: 853–64.

Sawer, Geoffrey. 1988. *The Australian Constitution*. Canberra: Australian Government Publishing Service.

Saylor, Thomas Reese. 1977. A New Legislative Mandate for American Food Aid. Pp. 199–211 in *Food Policy*, ed. Peter G. Brown and Henry Shue. New York: Free Press.

Schelling, Thomas C. 1960. *The Strategy of Conflict*. Cambridge, Mass.: Harvard University Press.

Schelling, Thomas C. 1971. On the Ecology of Micromotives. *Public Interest* 25: 61–98.

Schlesinger, Arthur M., Jr. 1957. *The Age of Roosevelt*. London: Heinemann.

Schwartz, Benjamin I. 1968. The Reign of Virtue: Some Broad Perspectives on Leader and Party in the Cultural Revolution. *The China Quarterly* 35: 1–17.

Scott, James C. 1972. *Comparative Political Corruption*. Englewood Cliffs, NJ: Prentice-Hall.

Scott, James C. 1976. *The Moral Economy of the Peasant*. New Haven, Conn.: Yale University Press.

Scott, Marvin B. and Lyman, Stanford M. 1968. Accounts. *American Sociological Review* 33: 46–63.

Selden, John. 1689. *Table Talk*. London: E. Smith.

Sen, Amartya. 1977. Rational Fools: A Critique of the Behavioral Foundations of Economic Theory. *Philosophy & Public Affairs* 6: 317–44.

Seneca Falls Woman's Rights Convention. 1848. Report of the Woman's Rights Convention Held at Seneca Falls, NY, July 19th and 20th, 1848. In *Woman's Rights Conventions, Seneca Falls & Rochester, 1848*. New York: Arno & the New York Times, 1969.

Shapley, L. S. 1967. On Solutions that Exclude One or More Players. Pp. 57–61 in *Essays in Mathematical Economics*, ed. Martin Shubik. Princeton, NJ: Princeton University Press.

Shklar, Judith. 1979. Let Us Not be Hypocritical. *Daedalus* 108 (3): 1–25.

Shue, Henry. 1980. *Basic Rights*. Princeton, NJ: Princeton University Press.

Sidgwick, Henry. 1883. *The Principles of Political Economy*. London: Macmillan.

Sidgwick, Henry. 1907. *The Methods of Ethics*. 7th edn. London: Macmillan.

Slovic, Paul; Fischhoff, Baruch; and Lichtenstein, Sarah. 1980. Facts versus Fears: Understanding Perceived Risk. In Kahneman, Slovic, and Tversky 1982, pp. 463–91.

Smith, Sidney. 1831. Four Speeches on the Reform Bill. Pp. 325–47 in *Selected Writings of Sydney Smith*, ed. W. H. Auden. London: Faber & Faber, 1957.

Smith, Sidney. 1839. Ballot. Pp. 347–67 in *Selected Writings of Sidney Smith*, ed. W. H. Auden. London: Faber & Faber, 1957.

Sniderman, Paul M.; Tetlock, Philip E.; Glaser, James M.; Green, Donald Philip; and Hout, Michael. 1989. Principled Tolerance and the American Mass Public. *British Journal of Political Science* 19: 47–67.

Spiro, Herbert J. 1959. *Government by Constitution*. New York: Random House.

Stampp, Kenneth M. 1964. *The Peculiar Institution: Negro Slavery in the American South*. London: Eyre & Spottiswoode.

Stanyer, Jeffrey. 1974. Divided Responsibilities: Accountability in Decentralized Government. *Public Administration Bulletin* 17: 14–30.

Stockman, David A. 1986. *The Triumph of Politics*. London: Bodley Head.

Stouffer, Samuel A. 1955. *Communism, Conformity and Civil Liberties*. New York: Doubleday.

Sullivan, John L.; Piereson, James; and Marcus, George E. 1982. *Political Toleration and American Democracy*. Chicago, Ill.: University of Chicago Press.

Sumner, William Graham. 1883. *What Social Classes Owe Each Other*. New York: Harper.

Sunstein, Cass R. 1988. Constitutions and Democracies: An Epilogue. Pp. 327–56 in *Constitutionalism and Democracy*, ed. Jon Elster and Rune Slagstrad. Cambridge: Cambridge University Press.

Taylor, E. 1971. *The House of Commons at Work*. 8th edn. Harmondsworth, Mddx: Penguin.

Taylor, Helen. 1867. The Claim of Englishwomen to the Suffrage Constitutionally Considered. Reprinted pp. 21–46 in *Before the Vote Was Won: Arguments For and Against the Women's Suffrage*, ed. Jane Lewis. New York: Routledge & Kegan Paul, 1987.

Taylor, Michael. 1969. Proof of a Theorem on Majority Rule. *Behavioral Science* 14: 228–31.

Taylor, Michael. 1982. *Community, Anarchy and Liberty*. Cambridge: Cambridge University Press.

Taylor, Michael. 1987. *The Possibility of Cooperation*. Cambridge: Cambridge University Press.

Taylor, Serge. 1984. *Making Bureaucracies Think: The Environmental Impact Statement Strategy of Administrative Reform*. Stanford, Calif.: Stanford University Press.

Thompson, Dennis F. 1987. *Public Ethics and Public Office*. Cambridge, Mass.: Harvard University Press.

Thompson, E. P. 1971. The Moral Economy of the English Crowd in the Eighteenth Century. *Past and Present* 50: 76–136.

Thompson, William. 1825. *Appeal of One Half of the Human Race, Women, Against the Pretensions of the Other Half, Men, to Retain Them in Political, and Thence in Civil and Domestic, Slavery*. London: Longman.

Thoreau, Henry David. 1848. Civil Disobedience. Pp. 27–50 in *Civil Disobedience: Theory and Practice*, ed. Hugo Adam Bedau. New York: Pegasus, 1969.

Titmuss, Richard M. 1950. *Problems of Social Policy*. Official Civil History of the Second World War. London: His Majesty's Stationery Office and Longman, Green.

Titmuss, Richard M. 1958a. The Social Division of Welfare: Some Reflections on the Search for Equity. Pp. 34–55 in *Essays on "the Welfare State."* London: Allen & Unwin.

Titmuss, Richard M. 1958b. War and Social Policy. Pp. 75–87 in *Essays on "the Welfare State."* London: Allen & Unwin.

Titmuss, Richard M. 1971. *The Gift Relationship*. London: Allen & Unwin.

Tocqueville, Alexis de. 1835. *Democracy in America*, trans. George

Lawrence, ed. J. P. Mayer and Max Lerner. New York: Harper & Row, 1966.

Torry, William I. 1986. Drought and the Government-Village Food Distribution System in India. *Human Organization* 45: 11–23.

Tulis, Jeffrey K. 1987. *The Rhetorical Presidency*. Princeton, NJ: Princeton University Press.

Tversky, Amos. 1977. Features of Similarity. *Psychological Review* 84: 327–52.

Tyler, Alice Felt. 1944. *Freedom's Ferment*. Minneapolis, Minn.: University of Minnesota Press.

Urmson, J. O. 1958. Saints and Heroes. Pp. 198–216 in *Essays in Moral Philosophy*, ed. A. I. Melden. Seattle, Wash.: University of Washington Press.

Vanberg, Viktor and Buchanan, James M. 1989. Interests and Theories in Constitutional Choice. *Journal of Theoretical Politics* 1: 49–62.

Waldron, Jeremy. 1988. When Justice Replaces Affection: The Need for Rights. *Harvard Journal of Law and Public Policy* 11: 625–47.

Walzer, Michael. 1983. *Spheres of Justice*. Oxford: Martin Robertson.

Walzer, Michael. 1989/90. A Critique of Philosophical Conversation. *Philosophical Forum* 21: 182–96.

Wasserstrom, Richard. 1964. Rights, Human Rights and Racial Discrimination. *Journal of Philosophy* 61: 628–41.

Weidenbaum, Murray L., chairman. 1982. Annual Report of the Council of Economic Advisers. In *Economic Report of the President, 1982*. Washington, DC: US Government Printing Office.

Wicksell, Knut. 1896. A New Principle of Just Taxation. Pp. 72–118 in *Classics in the Theory of Public Finance*, ed. Richard A. Musgrave and Alan T. Peacock. London: Macmillan, 1967.

Williams, Bernard. 1988. Formal Structures and Social Reality. Pp. 3–13 in *Trust*, ed. Diego Gambetta. Oxford: Blackwell.

Williamson, Chilton. 1960. *American Suffrage: From Property to Democracy, 1760–1860*. Princeton, NJ: Princeton University Press.

Wilson, James Q. 1990. Interests and Deliberation in the American Republic. *PS: Political Science & Politics* 23: 558–62.

Wilson, Woodrow. 1918. An Address to a Joint Session of Congress, January 8, 1918. Vol. 45, pp. 534–9 in *The Papers of Woodrow Wilson*, ed. Arthur S. Link. Princeton, NJ: Princeton University Press, 1984.

Wolfe, Tom. 1987. *The Bonfire of the Vanities*. New York: Farrar, Straus & Giroux.

Wood, Michael and Hughes, Michael. 1984. The Moral Basis of a Moral Reform: Status Discontent vs. Culture and Socialization as Explanations of Anti-Pornography Social Movement Adherence. *American Sociological Review* 49: 86–99.

Wyatt-Brown, Bertram. 1982. *Southern Honor: Ethics and Behavior in the Old South*. Oxford: Oxford University Press.

Zajac, Edward E. 1985. Perceived Economic Justice: The Example of Public Utility Regulation. Pp. 119–53 in *Cost Allocation: Methods, Principles, Applications*, ed. H. Peyton Young. Amsterdam: Elsevier.

Zeckhauser, Richard J. 1974. Risk Spreading and Distribution. Pp. 206–28 in *Redistribution Through Public Choice*, ed. Harold M. Hochman and George E. Peterson. New York: Columbia University Press.

Name Index

Subject Index

Index compiled by Jackie McDermott